Beyond the Body

Beyond the Body

An Antitheology of the Eucharist

James J. Heaney

PICKWICK *Publications* · Eugene, Oregon

BEYOND THE BODY
An Antitheology of the Eucharist

Copyright © 2014 James J. Heaney. All rights reserved. Except for brief quotations in critical publications or reviews, no part of this book may be reproduced in any manner without prior written permission from the publisher. Write: Permissions. Wipf and Stock Publishers, 199 W. 8th Ave., Suite 3, Eugene, OR 97401.

Pickwick Publications
An Imprint of Wipf and Stock Publishers
199 W. 8th Ave., Suite 3
Eugene, OR 97401

www.wipfandstock.com

ISBN 13: 978-1-62564-687-3

Cataloguing-in-Publication Data

Heaney, James J.

    Beyond the body : an antitheology of the Eucharist / James J. Heaney.

    xii + 158 p. ; 23 cm. Includes bibliographical references and index.

    ISBN 13: 978-1-62564-687-3

    1. Philosophy and religion. 2. Lord's Supper—Real presence. I. Title.

BV825.3 .H43 2014

Manufactured in the U.S.A.   09/23/2014

Unless otherwise noted, the scripture quotations contained herein are from the New Revised Standard Version of the Bible, copyright © 1989 the Division of Christian Education of the National Council of the Churches of Christ in the United States of America. Used by permission. All rights reserved.

For Elfriede

CONTENTS

Preface | ix

1 Introduction | 1
   Faith and Understanding
   "Anti-"Theology
   Eucharist

2 "This Is" and the Transience of Intelligibility | 15
   The Intelligible and the Interesting
   Universes of Understanding
   Two Paradigms
   Contrasting Ontologies
   The Anatomy of a Shift
   Paradigms and Doctrines

3 "Do This"—Text and Repetition | 44
   The Scandal of Hermeneutic Partisanship
   The Problem of the Poison Text
   The Letter that Gives Life
   Repetition
   The Moment
   A Postmodern Paradigm

4 Word and Deed | 73
   An Anatomy of Verbal Performance
   The Last Supper
   . . . of Many More

5 Beyond the Body | 106
    Two Types of Faith
    Two Types of Theology
    The Task of an Antitheology
    Alternate Criteria
    The Problem of "Presence"
    The Presence of Christ and the Presence of God
    Liturgy and Time

Bibliography | 147
Index | 155

PREFACE

This book takes its start from a conviction that faith is not something occasioned and initiated by either doctrine or theology but is rather a configuration of experience that comprises what is for each of us the world. As such it is the basis for a resident willingness to assent to statements drafted to represent publicly what faith is about, while keeping always in mind how slippery and provisional the interface between experience and attempts to describe it may be. The vocabulary ordinarily at our disposal to describe such a faith is either suspect or circular. To call it a "state of mind" requires agreement on what "mind" refers to or if, properly understood, whether there even is such a thing. "Intuition," representing as it does thought processes or events independent of rational argument, comes closer, but is largely restricted to assessing individual events or situations rather than the interrelated global apperceptions characteristic of the life of faith. "Outlook" is another helpful analogy, once we set aside that it refers mostly to prediction or expectation based on faith rather than on faith itself. Lastly, "conviction" speaks to the potential faith has for action but, again, this cannot exist without an objective corollary, a statement of what that conviction is *of*. Before doctrine and certainly before theology there is faith. What can we say about that faith as it directs itself to the Jesus who is the focus of the Eucharist?

The Western theological tradition, dominated by apologetic concerns since the thirteenth century, has with remarkable consistency maintained an order of business that makes a simple, unqualified, belief in the existence of God the intellectual preamble to everything else in matters of religion. The more rationalist side of that tradition left largely unsaid the implication that doctrines concerned with salvation, church, sacraments, and in this case the Eucharist, proceed from the doctrine of God in somewhat the same manner that the Son and the Spirit proceed from the Father in the

Preface

Trinity. Were God not to exist, none of these would make any sense; they are ultimately dependent upon that existence in both logical and practical terms. The more biblical side of that tradition is founded upon the great truths of salvation history but is guided by much the same conviction: a theology of redemption, including one of sacraments, would be senseless without a world and its resident humanity to redeem. It comes as no surprise, therefore that in the summas, institutes, and dogmatics of both traditions questions about sacraments, and the Eucharist in particular, come so much later in the agenda than everything else, the baggage of religion rather than its substance.

The imbalance of this first became clear to me quite by accident. A student, luckily someone else's student, asked about my work on this subject. Thinking primarily of the more demanding formulations of the doctrine of the Real Presence, I off-handedly replied that rather than a mystery it sometimes seemed more like a mystery story with a title like "The Case of the Poison Paradigm," in that, as I put it, "if you could believe this, you could believe anything." Setting aside the irreverence of this remark, it is clear that in some areas of belief the more demanding or dissonant the doctrine, the more it renders other, less demanding, claims more innocuous, turning the conventional order of argument on its head. Further, it is after all the "baggage" of religion that is the matter of its practice, and in the liturgy that is the focal point of that practice it is the Eucharist, not the Creed that has center stage. Again, students of comparative religion long ago noticed that deities of overall creation, whose existence was accepted but otherwise not much commented upon, tended to fade in importance unless local circumstance required their recall. It is not for nothing, therefore, that both Luther and Calvin insisted as they did upon the regular celebration of the Eucharist. Faith in the Eucharist, far from being a theological afterthought, has a major role in keeping faith in God alive.

Readers familiar with the literature of religion will recognize that although flying under a literary flag of convenience as an "antitheology," this is a work of philosophical theology. Thinking that philosophy grants too little that is of importance and that theology grants too much that is not, the philosophical theologian generally aims at producing results friendly to both camps without subscribing completely to either. This is sometimes viewed cynically by critics as falling between the proverbial two stools, the best response to which is that between both may well be where the most solid ground is to be found. Aspiring to be neither a philosophy of religion

Preface

nor a "fundamental" theology, philosophical theology nevertheless does harbor some foundational ambitions. In this case its primary interests are in uncovering the most elemental presuppositions of belief in the Eucharist, particularly as these are evident in the nature of doctrine, the role of text, and the use of that text in religious practice. Should this seem a little enough return for the extent of investment involved, it would be good to recall that the basics of religion live primarily in the less elaborate beliefs of the pew rather than in those of the seminary or the university.

The catalyst for undertaking this task was, quite simply, the dividedness that currently characterizes both Christianity and public life. Although several of the older mainline denominations have authorized intercommunion among their members, technical disagreement still exists in their positions on the Eucharist. This is saddening, since differences like these are likely at some point to out, regardless of how long dormant they may have lain. Whether one accepts that there is a Real Presence of some sort in the Eucharist or denies it in favor of an act that identifies and binds together the community of the saved, it nonetheless remains for all the paramount event in the life of faith, the token of membership in *all* the mysteries, and the most constant reminder of belief in a life to come. It would be unrealistic to hope that the notion of Eucharistic presence proposed here would be so acceptable to all as to render any others mere adiaphora, matters of only local importance, but if it manages to at least suggest a new avenue of exploration toward unity that will have been enough.

The pages that follow represent the completion of a journey, one in which many had a part. My most sincere thanks go to Derwood Smith, former chair and current colleague, for bringing me to Cleveland State University, to the kind of teaching that has been my heart's lifelong desire. Of the helpfulness of the university's Michael Schwartz library one cannot say enough, from interlibrary loan to the wonderful convenience of the OhioLINK program, through which the resources of university libraries and seminaries of every sort across the state are readily available. The immense holdings of the Cleveland Public Library, founded as the people's university, are an additional never-ending source of joy for their depth and contemporaneity. I am particularly grateful to it for access to *The Whole Works of Jeremy Taylor*.

Students down the years have been a constant source of inspiration and encouragement. Their passion for understanding and their unquenchable curiosity have both made me proud and humbled me at the opportunity

Preface

to work with them. Dr. Louanne K. Bachner, Conor Malloy, Rev. Pamela Rumancik, and Nicholas Boros in particular remain for me always as landmarks in both life and thought. As a constant conversation partner I have also been privileged to share difficulties encountered at several points in the book with Rev. Brian Shields of the Cleveland Clinic, whose pastoral commonsense and listening skills invariably prompted ways to a solution. Several such points were also first aired to the adult study groups of the Church of the Saviour (United Methodist) and Bethlehem Lutheran Church, both of Cleveland Heights, Ohio. I am especially grateful to my daughter, Cordelia Heaney, for editorial advice on how to keep literary elegance and intelligibility from becoming strangers to each other. Lastly, more than I can say I thank my wife, Elfriede, to whom this book is dedicated.

1

INTRODUCTION

Faith and Understanding

A century before the intellectual upheavals that would culminate in the "scholastic" theology and philosophy of the great medieval universities, Anselm, later to become archbishop of Canterbury, set out to determine what certainty might attach to our most elemental notions of God.[1] He did this from the standpoint of one doubting not God but the sufficiency of human understanding for describing God, either as such or as the object of human religious feelings, attitudes, and expectations. Although the motive for Anselm's quest has been widely construed as a need for assurance that God does in fact exist and has on this reading sponsored an enormous literature of both agreement and disagreement, more yet remains to be said regarding the shape of this program as he characterized it: *fides quaerens intellectum*, "faith seeking understanding."[2]

The seeming simplicity of this triad of terms easily tempts the reader, whether casual or professional, to assume their meanings to be readily available either in the text of Anselm's work, in its religious and cultural contexts, or, more ambitiously perhaps, in those forms or instances of thinking within in it that typify human reason. And the breadth and depth

---

1. Born in Aosta, northern Italy, around 1033, Anselm became the abbot of the French monastery of Bec in 1078 and served as archbishop of Canterbury from 1093 until his death in 1109.

2. Anselm's most complete statement of this principle is to be found in his "On the Incarnation of the Word" in *Major Works*, 235–38.

of scholarship on Anselm bear ample witness to the wealth of possibilities for interpretation these offer. But although Anselm influenced a few in his time whom we might think of as followers, no "Anselmian" school would develop as there would be schools of Thomists, Scotists, Calvinists, Kantians, Heideggerians, or even Lonerganians in later centuries. In part this is owing to Anselm's predilection for writing directly about the matters in hand without any seeming need to prove his consistency with the written tradition. In the letter to his former teacher Lanfranc introducing his first great effort, the *Monologion*, he attributes this directness to his own lack of education.[3] But the absence of ostentatious erudition throughout his works fails to hide that it is not the words but the thoughts and convictions of his predecessors that he has so completely taken to heart and understood that he prefers to express them as *he* sees them rather than citing them supportively in proof texts. Debts to predecessors he certainly has, the greatest of these to Augustine, like whom he employs whatever genre or style suits the purpose in hand, whether monolog, dialog, letter, prayer, or topically focused treatise. And further like Augustine, it is his style that carries the discussion forward, in a carefully orchestrated flow of words that conjointly express the sought-for understanding, words that find their meaning within that flow rather than in external definition.

That Anselm left no school behind, no metaphysical system that could be adapted to explore further areas of the theological landscape, is hardly a fault, considering the extent of his effect on later Western religious thought. His description of Christ's redemptive action as substitutionary atonement in *Why God Became Man* remains central to the theology and religious life of Reformed Christianity in the Calvinist tradition. His eloquence on the sinless purity of Mary in the conception of Jesus and the unique role this defines for her as intermediary between God and humanity has similarly shaped centuries of Roman Catholic devotion and theological thought alike. His "ontological" argument for the existence of God, perhaps more an accidental than an intended outcome of his efforts, seems never to fall from favor as an object of contentious philosophical interest. And, of course, that faith seeks understanding has over the centuries come to represent both the most convincing motive for the enterprise of theological investigation and the surest test of its religious sincerity.

Curiously, the durability of Anselm's religious and intellectual legacy is in some measure guaranteed by the nearly limitless openness it offers

---

3. "Letter to Archbishop Lanfranc," in *Major Works*, 3–4.

Introduction

to interpretation. His argument for the existence of God, for instance, has been viewed as variously as an exercise in logic, a key to mystical experience, a theological exegesis of the divine name, and a species of "Christian gnosticism."[4] That such varied construals are at all possible, however, raises the reasonable suspicion that there is something vague or insufficiently clear about Anselm's intent, something more fundamental than those natural differences about understanding historical materials most commonly occasioned by the personal interests of interpreters, the increasing sophistication of critical analysis, or the discovery of new texts. And yet Anselm, as the most detailed scholarship shows, seems remarkably clear, coherent, and consistent in his thinking wherever we look, both within individual works and across the span of his writing as a whole.[5]

One possibility for understanding this seeming contradiction between an overall intent that is difficult to pin down and an unassailable clarity of presentation can be found in the level of generalization involved. In logic, the less specific the meanings or references of terms in a statement, the more widely applicable it will be. The upside of such statements is their great "power" or range of description. The downside is their lack of specificity. The injunction to "do good and avoid evil," for instance, provides exemplary encouragement to ethical behavior but speaks not at all to what we may think is good or evil in any given situation. Similarly, on the face of it "faith seeking understanding" appears to provide a comprehensive and principled description of theological inquiry, almost an algorithm for it, to which few, if any could object, yet it assumes much but says little about either faith, understanding, or the nature of the quest. The charm this exerts derives in part from the opportunity it allows for each of those terms to resonate with the personal interests or experience of the reader. Such an approach to texts, it should not be forgotten, had long been institutionalized in the medieval world through the practice of *lectio divina*, a free-associating approach to reading Scripture that encouraged calling to mind whatever other texts might serve to illuminate for the reader a given text under consideration.

It is difficult to put a limit on the number of possible ways that "faith" can be understood in the theological tradition. For Anselm, where doctrine

---

4. As noted in Fairweather, *A Scholastic Miscellany,* 49–53. The views characterized by Fairweather are philosophical logic (his own), mysticism (Anselm Stolz), theology (Karl Barth), and Christian Gnosticism (Etienne Gilson).

5. Hopkins, *Companion,* 3–5.

is its object faith consists in the assent to a particular set of authorized propositions about God, world, soul, salvation, and more. Some of these may be understood completely, others less so because of the disproportion between the human ability to know and their divine object. Propositional faith is of itself thus necessarily incomplete, requiring the willing suspension of disbelief in things that cannot be known, including future events in the history of salvation.[6] But how, exactly, is such a faith to "seek" understanding other than to improve its parsing of propositions or to hope for future experience to fill in the gaps? While mystical experience would seem to qualify as a solution, it is not clear that indescribable experience of an indescribable object can be scripted to fulfill the requirements of understanding. And although Anselm's devotional writing rises to a high level of eloquence, there is little if any evidence in it of contact with the literature of the mystical tradition.[7] His advice on what to do where the demands of the language of faith exceed the capacities of reason is quite mundane: "A Christian should advance through faith to understanding, not come to faith through understanding, or withdraw from faith if he cannot understand. Rather, when he is able to attain to understanding, he is delighted; but when he cannot, he reveres what he is not able to grasp."[8]

If faith is expressed or acted upon in assent to propositions, even those we cannot fully understand, what is faith when not thus occupied? The hub of this dilemma, that faith is somehow prior to and different from moments in speech that confess it appears in Anselm's initial statement about the aims of his second great project, the *Proslogion*, and its proof of the existence of God: "Well, then, Lord, You who give understanding to faith, grant me that I may understand, as much as you see fit, that You exist as we believe You to exist, and that You are as we believe You to be." Lest there be any ambiguity regarding what this might be, he further qualifies: "Now we believe that you are something than which nothing greater can be thought."[9]

---

6. Anselm sees a proposition as having two sorts of truth. One is in the grammatical and logical correctness of its formulation. The other is the truth of the references it makes. Propositions that state matters of faith can therefore be responsibly assented to as true, even though incompletely understood. "Concerning Truth (*De Veritate*)," in *Truth, Freedom, and Evil*, 12–18, 92–96.

7. Hopkins, *Companion*, 34–36.

8. "To Bishop Fulco of Beauvais (Epistola 136)" in Anselm, *Trinity, Incarnation, and Redemption*, 4.

9. "Proslogion," in Anselm, *Major Works*, 87, translating "Ergo, domine, qui das fidei intellectum, da mihi, ut quantum scis expedire intelligam, quia es sicut credimus, et hoc

Introduction

Considerable theological attention has been devoted to the condition Anselm places on this process, that it must enable us to understand God *quod credimus,* as we believe God to be.[10] Less noticed is that this is not the God of creed or church but the one stipulated in the *Monologion,* an object of thought of such nature than we cannot in principle think of any that could be superior (*maius*) to it. Such a concept and the fact of its being expressed, however, are not faith itself but the understanding of it as verbally realized. What is required as both inspiration of and justification for such a statement is a lived experience of things related to each other in ways that make a comparison of such broad generality possible. At the outset of the *Monologion* Anselm sets this within a question:

> Given that there is such an uncountable number of good things, the sheer multiplicity of which is simply a datum of bodily sense as well as something we perceive by the rational mind—given this, are we to believe that there is some one thing through which all good things whatever are good?[11]

The perception of these good things that antedates the verbally expressed understanding of faith is, simply, faith itself. The list of topics to be considered with which the *Monologion* begins provides an indication of their range: from the swiftness of a horse to the wonder of createdness, from the fact of physical existence to the destiny of the soul, from the intimation of a supreme good to the notion of a triune God exemplifying internally both the good and the love of it that is the force behind faith's quest for understanding.

At first sight it might seem that Anselm is here merely prefiguring in a less structured manner Aquinas's fourth way to the existence of God, from "the gradation observed in things." But Aquinas is less concerned with the perception of good than with the support that this perceived gradation provides for the existence of a sequence of causes that could not be at all

---

es quod credimus. Et quidem credimus te esse aliquid quo nihil maius cogitari possit" (Anselm, *Opera Omnia,* 1:101).

10. In particular Karl Barth, *Anselm,* 13 and passim.

11. Anselm, *Major Works,* 11. "Cum tamen innumerabilia bona sint, quorum tam multam, diversitatem et sensibus corporeis experimur et ratione mentis discernimus: estne credendum esse unum aliquid, per quo unum sint bona quæcumque bona sunt, an sunt bona alia per aliud?" (Anselm, *Opera Omnia,* 1:14).

were there no first, initiating, cause. This latter Aquinas identifies simply by appeal to linguistic commonplace: "this we call 'God.'"[12]

The contrast between Aquinas and Anselm on this could not be more stark. The world of the Five Ways is one of an unknowably extensive sequence of causal events the most determinative feature of which is that it cannot in principle be infinite. Even in the fifth way, predicating a governing intelligence behind the guidedness of nature, the name "God" is once more assigned to that something primarily out of deference to the common usage of the term.[13]

Perhaps the most definitive difference between these is that Anselm's world of good things, including as it does not only physical objects but immaterial ones like thoughts, justice, and even truth itself,[14] is a world that exists and is perceived in the present. For Anselm it is simply what is the case, as Wittgenstein would later express much the same perception.[15] For Aquinas both world and theology are strikingly more remote, a virtually unknowable train of events or relationships that are only in principle finite, dependent on linguistic custom and logic for meaning rather than immediate apprehension. For Anselm the real task of understanding is to render in language the perceived world that is faith.

"Anti-"Theology

Religion, and by extension theology, has most often found its greatest opponents in the ranks of the philosophers. This is by no means surprising, considering the hermeneutic of suspicion that has often driven philosophy to question the most basic givens in culture, particularly those pertaining to religion, politics, and ethics, and, when these were not enough, reality in general. Religion has been pilloried by philosophy for its use of fear as a tool to cow its adherents (Lucretius), the ridiculousness of its sacramental practices (Hume), unenlightened self-interest as the ethic of its clergy (Kant), suppression of economic dissent through the promise of heaven (Marx), and the meaninglessness of its most basic assertions (Logical

---

12. ST 1a.2.3. References throughout the present volume are from the McGraw Hill edition, cited according to convention by part, question, and article, e.g., ST. 3a.74,2.

13. Ibid., 70. "Ergo est aliquid intelligens, a quo omnes res naturales ordinantur ad finem, et hoc dicimus Deum" (Thomas, Aquinas, *Corpus Thomisticum*).

14. Anselm, *Truth, Freedom, and Evil*, 91.

15. "Die Welt is alles was der Fall ist" (Wittgenstein, *Tractatus*, 6).

Introduction

Positivism), to name but a few. Despite their trenchant opposition to religion and to theology as its intellectual outrider, however, each of these bears its own cargo of grand assumptions about the world, ones weighty enough and broadly applicable enough to grace them with at least some of what they find reprehensible in religion. Such assumptions range from a naïve acceptance of an all-encompassing materialism to a dubious belief in the all-sufficiency of intellectual clarity for satisfactory understanding. While these may not qualify as "talk of God," each reflects in some way a set of convictions that in other times and places were undeniably theological, whether as devotional pantheism, the worship of reason as *logos*, or belief in a dialectical dualism as the engine of events. Disbelief in religion all too easily masks the presence of a theology in another guise.

This critical recognition of the tendency of philosophy in general, and of some essentially skeptical philosophers in particular, to assume too much of a grander, metaphysical nature has given rise from time to time to what French philosopher Alain Badiou calls "antiphilosophy."[16] Among the antiphilosophers he counts Pascal for his exposure of the soulless rationalism of Descartes, Nietzsche for his destructive critique of Plato, Kierkegaard for his dethroning of Hegel, and Wittgenstein for his insistence that philosophy must somehow divest itself of itself to attain the level of understanding to which it aspires. Although not himself a believer, Badiou also admiringly includes the apostle Paul in this list for having rejected Jewish particularity in framing Christianity as a universal religion.[17] Among the leading characteristics of an antiphilosophy he lists first of all a critique of the statements of philosophy on a logical, linguistic, and "genealogical" basis that amounts to "a deposing of the category of truth." Of itself, this further requires we recognize that philosophy cannot be reduced simply to a fabric of propositions. And finally, the act that is philosophy must be replaced, transcended, not by announcing a new set of propositions but by a new antiphilosophical act that "consists in letting what there is show itself."[18]

Applying these criteria to theology, several figures emerge as antitheologians. The Pietist movement of the seventeenth century, for instance, conscientiously rejected the doctrinal controversialism of the Reformation in favor of an emphasis on Christian life and practice, a position

---

16. Badiou, *Wittgenstein's Antiphilosophy*, 75. Badiou attributes the first use of this term to Jacques Lacan.

17. Ibid., 69.

18. Ibid., 75–76, 80.

exemplified in Johann Arndt's *True Christianity* (1606). Following Arndt, Pietism in general held fairly negative views of church structure, formal theology, and even the sacraments, lodging the possibility of salvation in a life of devotion. Similar tendencies appeared simultaneously in English-speaking Protestantism in a range of figures from Jeremy Taylor, whose *Rule and Exercise of Holy Living* (1650) remains a classic of the spiritual life, to Jonathan Edwards's *Treatise Concerning Religious Affections* (1746), which attempted to reestablish Christian piety on an epistemological basis distinct from those of either pietistic emotionalism or radical rationalism. Pascal's fascination with theological issues and his opposition to theological formalism are as well known as his criticism of Descartes, and the singularity of Kierkegaard's philosophical stance often obscures the theological ambition of much of his work. And if being a contrarian is at all a mark of the antitheologian, one need hardly look further than D. F. Strauss, whose *Life of Jesus* (1835) effected what would later become an occupational separation of biblical criticism from formal theology. In the twentieth century, the works of Pierre Teilhard de Chardin, publishable only after his death in 1955, implicitly rejected the scholastic orthodoxy entrenched in Roman Catholicism since the Reformation for an evolutionary religious Neoplatonism fully attuned to modern science. What unites these, and other similar figures in the history of theology we might think of, is that they hold basic experience intellectually prior to statements about it, recognize both the communal authority of doctrinal statements and their necessarily provisional character in relation to experience, and consider faith to be an act of perception that must be ever new and original.

While casting Anselm as a type of the antitheologian is anachronistic in that the cultural separation of philosophy from theology would not become institutionalized until more than a century after his death, his insistence on beginning from basic perceptions rather than from texts very much marks him as such. Well trained and accomplished in the primarily syllogistic technique of argument then known as dialectic, he nevertheless cedes to it only an authority well below that of scripture or tradition and demonstrates a prescient distaste for any theological inquiry that puts matters of faith in doubt: "For it is utterly foolish and pointless to bring back into the uncertainty of puzzling questions what is firmly established on solid rock—to do so at the behest of every man who lacks understanding."[19] As age and ecclesiastical preferment led the Anselm who as a monastic teacher

---

19. Anselm, *Trinity, Incarnation, and Redemption*, 4.

Introduction

had written the *Monologion* and the *Proslogion* for his students to the more publicly visible position of Archbishop of Canterbury, the questions that occupied him became correspondingly more doctrinal. His later works are topical, written at request and frequently interventionary, particularly where established doctrines like the Trinity, the Incarnation, and the Virgin Birth are at stake. His announced estimate of his own ability to take up such tasks is invariably modest but puts us on notice thereby that the efforts to be made will be entirely his own. The most noticeable difference from his earlier works is that in addition to the fundamental perceptions to which those appealed he is now able, thanks to the arguments put forward in "Concerning Truth" (*de Veritate*), to count among them greater abstractions like truth in itself, as well as it is to be seen in acts, the justice of acts, and even in the essence of things.[20]

Anselm is generally regarded as having little of consequence to say about the doctrine of the Eucharist, being primarily interested in "the symbolism rather than the efficacy"[21] of the sacrament. And, as it happens, his "Letters on the Sacraments" appear to show no interest at all in either the controversy over the Eucharist that had so preoccupied his teacher Lanfranc or the panoply of technical questions about physical location, corruptibility, sacramental effect, and miracle raised by his contemporary Guitmund of Aversa, whose treatise on the subject established the catalog of such issues for centuries to come.[22] This lack of interest may, of course, represent nothing more than a recognition by Anselm that the heavy lifting on this topic had already been done, but it witnesses eloquently as well to an extraordinary caution in handling controversial questions.

The setting for the letters is the Great Schism, beginning in 1054, that divided the churches of the Latin West from their Greek counterparts. Anselm was involved on several fronts in addressing theological points related to the division. The announced subject of the letters is disagreement over whether leavened or unleavened bread should be used in the Eucharist. As Anselm frames the dispute, the Greeks seem to believe that the West's use of unleavened bread adds an unnecessarily interpretive dimension to sacramental practice, favoring Jewish usage in the Passover ritual over the

---

20. Anselm, *Three Philosophical Dialogues*, 96–103.

21. Anselm, *Trinity, Incarnation, and Redemption*, xv. See also Evans, *Anselm*, 103–5.

22. Vaillancourt, *Lanfranc of Canterbury and Guidmund of Aversa*. Both wrote in response to the claim of Berengar of Tours (ca. 1010–1088) that the lack of a proper referent for "this" in "this is my body" entailed that it could only be taken in a figurative sense.

Beyond the Body

declaration of Jesus in John 6:35 that he is the bread of life, where only ordinary, not ritual, bread would surely have been meant. Anselm's response to this is simply that at the Last Supper Jesus enjoined on his followers an act of remembrance rather than a ritual protocol, saying "do this," not "Do what I am doing with that which I am doing it." His ultimate solution to the problem of differences in ritual is that "in performing divine actions we ought to use what we deem to be more worthy."[23]

But although in the letters Anselm addresses none of those issues that so fascinated Lanfranc and Guitmund, closer inspection reveals a carefully phrased, though guarded, position on the Eucharist quite distinct from theirs, set within a structure of inquiry governed by the principle that faith seeks understanding. Conspicuously absent is any mention of the notion of substance as a descriptor for either the elements of bread and wine or the body and blood of Christ. Freed of the necessity to refer to objects in general as only visible manifestations of an adamantly persistent substratum,[24] he is able to refer to these particular objects simply as what they are said to be in the context of the liturgy rather than as physical entities undergoing a mysterious change of invisible being. For Anselm, Jesus at the Last Supper "produced" his body from bread,[25] just as does the celebrant in the consecration of the mass.[26] There is no agonizing over what sort of change might bring this about, questioning why the properties of bread and wine are still in evidence, or even any expression of wonder relating to the event.

The reason for this lack of interest in such obvious questions becomes clearer when we recall Anselm's description of the process of faith seeking understanding: "when he is able to attain to understanding, he is delighted; but when he cannot, he reveres what he is not able to grasp."[27] The process starts not with theological argument but with the same sort of basic perception that belief in God did, except that now it refers to the event that is the speaking of the words of institution, "this is my body." Although it is

---

23. Anselm, "Letters on the Sacraments: The Sacrifice of Leavened and Unleavened Bread" in *Trinity, Incarnation, and Redemption*, 138. Cf. *Opera Omnia*, 2:226-27.

24. Although the fully metaphysical character of the notion of substance would only become clear in the later recovery of the works of Aristotle, Guitmund's use of "substantialiter transmutatur" certainly anticipates it (Vaillancourt, *Lanfranc of Canterbury*, 117).

25. Anselm, *Trinity, Incarnation, and Redemption*, 136. Cf. "Et cum legitur de domino, quando corpus suum de pane *fecit*" (Anselm, *Opera Omnia* 2:223-24, italics mine).

26. Ibid., 137. Cf. "... pane, de quo carnem ipsum *conficimus*" (Anselm, *Opera Omnia*, 2:225, italics mine).

27. Anselm, *Trinity, Incarnation, and Redemption*, 4.

Introduction

beyond our understanding, we can still acknowledge, as Anselm says, "the truth of the thing itself,"[28] just as we can acknowledge the truth of other things as well. Once we have done that, we have reached the highest degree of understanding possible to us. What remains is to venerate, to worship, in the way we deem most worthy. Anselm's interest in "symbol rather than efficacy" is based, thus, not on aesthetic considerations but on fidelity to what he believes to be the truth of the Eucharist. Much of what seems in the letters like manneristic fussing over the symbolism of very minor actions in the liturgy is really an exploration of how to decide among reasonable differences in practice while remaining faithful to that truth.

For all his efforts to defend the institutional church of his time and its inherited doctrines, Anselm nonetheless stands as an idiosyncratic thinker whose work, no matter how inspired by his predecessors, remained completely his own. It may seem bold to the point of reckless to mention him beside Nietzsche, whose announced philosophical ambition was "To break in two the history of the world,"[29] but we cannot deny the liminal position that Anselm occupies in Western thought in general and medieval thought in particular. Despite his frequent characterizationa as the last of the early medievals and the first of the scholastics, he somehow manages resolutely to be neither of these.

Eucharist

Over the past century and a half, the liturgy of the Eucharist has become increasingly central to the devotional life of Christian churches, particularly those committed to a "real presence" of Christ realized when the words of Jesus at the Last Supper are ritually repeated. The formal terms and conditions of that presence vary widely, from the unyielding insistence on a real, though undetectable, alteration of bread and wine into body and blood enshrined in the term "transubstantiation" to less off-putting but no less intellectually demanding allusions to that presence as "in, with, and under" what is seen.[30] The dual sources of renewed emphasis on the Eucharist were

---

28. Ibid., 149–50; "rei veritate" (Anselm, *Opera Omnia*, 2:240).

29. Cited in Badiou, *Wittgenstein's Antiphilosophy*, 76.

30. As commonly phrased in the Lutheran tradition. A great variety of moderating positions allow for the bread and wine to remain unchanged. *The Oxford Dictionary of the Christian Church*, 3rd ed., s.v. "consubstantiation," "receptionism," "virtualism," the last of these attributed to John Calvin. For an excellent overview see Hunsinger,

Beyond the Body

the liturgical movement that originated in Roman Catholicism and the ecumenical movement among Protestant churches that enabled a positive revaluing of some aspects of the Western tradition that the Reformation had dismissed out of hand.

A shadowy accompaniment to this new interest in the Eucharist was the growth of an individual piety directed not to the physical elements of the sacrament but to a felt personal presence of Christ occasioned by, but certainly not identified with them. Whether this was an effect of the intellectual individualism of the Enlightenment, the emotional personalism of Romanticism, or the rise of psychology as a medical discipline is open to speculation. As a development in the life of faith it was broadly welcomed, despite the evident lack of any support for it in the Roman tradition which had, since Anselm's time, remained unwaveringly committed to a metaphysics of change as sufficient explanation. In some churches descended from the Calvinist wing of the Reformation that were strongly opposed to the notion of Real Presence, having "a real relation to the person of Christ" gradually became a defining quality for the faithful spiritual life. For other churches historically allied to the pietist tradition, the person of Christ in such a relationship supplies all the Eucharistic presence that is required.[31]

Owing to the intellectual incompatibility of medieval notions of substance with the understanding of objects around us that is common today, realist or "physicalist" views of the Eucharist demand that we believe something essentially unintelligible to us. The unreasonableness of the demand is further reinforced by the now widely declared end of metaphysics as an enterprise of philosophy.[32] With regard to the Eucharist, this is not a matter of mystery or of disproportion between knower and would-be known, but simply of being able to make sense of a claim that so uncompromisingly contradicts our ordinary experience of the logic of identity. And given this, there is no likelihood that such a mystery could ever in principle be resolved, even in the vision of the blessed in heaven.

Replacing a realist notion of presence with a highly personal, emotionally related, one, however, is likewise not without its contemporary

---

Eucharist, 21–46.

31. "United Methodists, along with other Christian traditions, have tried to provide clear and faithful interpretations of Christ's presence in the Holy Meal. Our tradition asserts the real, personal, living presence of Jesus Christ." See http://www.umc.org/site/apps/nlnet/content.aspx?c=lwL4KnN1LtH&b=5070513&ct=3334393.

32. Most prominently Wrathall, *Religion after Metaphysics*; Manoussakis, *God after Metaphysics*; and Hector, *Theology Without Metaphysics*.

Introduction

risks. Since Freud the mystery surrounding motive and its sources has done much to erode any certainty we might have that the character of the person of Christ we think to encounter is completely independent of manufacture by unknown forces within our own personalities. Yet more difficult, the demise of metaphysics similarly threatens even the very concepts that Freud depended upon, those concerned with the existence of a perduring ego, person, and self-identity, by no means as clear and seemingly well founded as they once were. Can there be a clear a notion of the person of Christ when so little is clear about the human person to begin with?

The basic task of an antitheology is an essentially descriptive one. It begins at the working face of every difficulty by looking, as simply and directly as possible, at what is the case, what assumptions, perceptions, intuitions, lie unquestioned and even unmentioned in a faith not yet spoken aloud in explanation. Together these comprise what is, intellectually, the world of faith, that point from which the pursuit of understanding embarks. The purposeful delineation of that world is by no means a hostile act propelled by doubt, but one searching with reverence and respect for the most elemental footings of belief. The ultimate task of the pages that follow is to describe the intellectual footprint of a nonmetaphysical Eucharistic faith.

A first essential area of investigation is the relationship of what we believe to what we *say* we believe. What intellectual claim can historical doctrines have on us? Theological doctrines, much like scientific ones, are products of their originating periods and can best, perhaps even only, be understood on that basis. There are quite reasonable grounds to conclude that what may have made a great deal of sense in the ninth century would become increasingly less intelligible when later encumbered by specifically Aristotelian notions of substance.

If doctrines are more like end-nodes on the branches of a diverse evolutionary process than moments in a progressive revelation or realization, is religious doctrine not then hopelessly relativized? Text, the specific case in point being that of the New Testament Last Supper account, is far more durable than any doctrines derived from it. But text, as Plato pointed out in the *Phaedrus*, is also unstable in its effects. Looking to the analysis of repetition initiated by Kierkegaard, the meaning of a text, despite its material permanence, is realized only where its spoken repetition transcends redundancy to constitute a unique and unrepeatable moment.

Beyond the Body

But "do this in remembrance of me" is a very particular type of text, a command or request of the sort the British philosopher J. L. Austin called a "performative utterance." It is in the presuppositions necessary for such utterances to be successful that John Searle and Jürgen Habermas, following Austin, find a social "world" or "lifeworld" of the persons involved in performative transactions. The lifeworld of liturgical utterances like "do this in remembrance of me," however, is not simply social but also epistemic. In it such moments occur not as normal, routine, or ordinary happenings, but as interventionary, transformative events of the sort described by Alan Badiou.

Stepping aside from traditional approaches to Eucharistic doctrine will have been worth it only if this results in a characterization of Eucharistic belief that both meets the needs of and can be fruitful for the further development of religious life in general. Where traditional rationalizing and scriptural theologies succeed as explanatory vehicles for the public language of faith, they fail to touch those basic aspects of religious experience that are the most real, the most immediate, and the most personal. The practical goal of the pages that follow is to refocus Eucharistic piety on the liturgical act itself as a transformative event united in time with the person of Jesus in both remembrance and thanksgiving.

2

"THIS IS" AND THE TRANSIENCE OF INTELLIGIBILITY

> But what seems reasonable or unreasonable changes.
> What in certain ages seems reasonable in others seems not.
> —WITTGENSTEIN, *On Certainty*[1]

The Intelligible and the Interesting

We can never really know what the historical Jesus was thinking when he uttered the words "This is my body," and this for many reasons. The simplest, perhaps, is rooted in our ineluctable differences from each other as individuals. We understand others, as Augustine suggested, based on our understanding of ourselves, but we cannot ever walk perfectly in their shoes. A range of human intellectual enterprises from metaphysical philosophies to modern social sciences have tried to bridge this gap with larger-than-life concepts like "human nature" and the "normal." We flee to these when the difficulties of mutual understanding become too great, or when we want

---

1. From the German text: "Aber was Menschen vernünftig oder unvernünftig erscheint, ändert sich. Zu gewißen Zeiten scheint Menschen etwas vernünftig, was zu andern Zeiten unvernünftig schien" (Wittgenstein, *On Certainty*, 43).

to lighten the burdens of individuality by painting them as "problems that everyone has." But at the heart of generalizations like these is primarily an underlying preference for the ontological riskiness of reasoning by analogy over the threatening isolation of emotional and intellectual solipsism.

A less programmatic but more direct source of difficulty is the intractability of the words themselves. On the face of it, they constitute logically nothing more than an intended self reference that fails because it points to something other than the speaker's own body. As a stark departure from the ordinary conventions of self-referring language use with which we are familiar, this certainly qualifies as a *différance*, a "show stopper," but curiously not one based on any actual "difference" we can detect. Nothing, for example that would qualify as an "intervention" has occurred, since, for instance, no explicit claim is made in the New Testament text that "this" *is not* or *is no longer* bread, nor is there any hint of an action, an event, a verbal formula, responsible for a change. And there is no indication in the words that they are used in any familiar nonreferring way like metaphor, figure, image, or allegory. To all intents and appearances "this is" leaves us stranded on a solecism.

Where biblical studies in the nineteenth and twentieth centuries often tried to resolve problems of meaning in the New Testament by appeal to common standards of reason, history, language, and society, the contemporary breakdown of the liberal consensus on human nature and destiny and the concomitant distrust of historical and scientific method as routes to truth have closed down those courts of appeal, perhaps even for good. Bereft of universally applicable interpretive tools, we find ourselves strangers in what was once a familiar historical landscape, forced to confront each new challenge as though the world had yet to be discovered. But although the intellectual discomforts of this situation are certainly considerable, there are still undeniable advantages in returning to presuppositionless critique as a starting point. Perhaps the greatest of these is the obligation to let things simply be what they are in themselves, rather than allowing them meaning only in the context of larger, primarily narrative, frameworks. But this means meeting texts like "this is" and events like the last supper as aliens to our experience, as residents of "lifeworlds" we may know only through them. If there were a Kantian category for this kind of knowledge, it would likely be the one proposed by Kierkegaard, the "interesting."[2] In

---

2. Kierkegaard, writing as pseudoauthor "Johannes de Silentio," *Fear and Trembling*, 109–10, 121. In Kierkegaard's telling of this venerable folk tale, the maid Agnes is irresistibly seduced by the Merman's difference from anything in her prior experience.

"This Is" and the Transience of Intelligibility

terms of any results we might anticipate, the familiar and the ordinary are out of the question. We find ourselves rather, as Clifford Geertz once put it, committed to ferreting out the anomalous and the strange, becoming in the process perhaps not so much scholars as "merchants of astonishment."[3]

But should it not strike us as odd that our near-fatal and seemingly universalizable difficulties with "this is" as a putative factual assertion have not been shared by everyone, everywhere in the Western religious tradition? The absence of this phrase from the supper account in the gospel of John leaves open, of course, the suggestion of a disagreement between that gospel and the tradition represented by the synoptics and 1 Corinthians, but there are no historical means available to us for reliably determining whether this was so. Yet certainly the authors/redactors of the synoptics felt no need to qualify the words as problematic, nor did they ascribe any intellectual diffidence to Jesus in using them. The setting for the words is undeniably dramatic in intention and electrifying in effect, but not suggestive of either literary nuance or judicious phrasing. The text makes no effort to hedge its bets with either history or philosophy. It says what it says Jesus said, nothing more.

The silence of the New Testament about what seems to us a painful quandary was generally left undisturbed throughout the early Christian centuries and the late Latin West. Various figures, Ambrose most prominent among them, considered "this is," without either tremor or hesitation, to be a reference to the physical body of Jesus in the sacrament.[4] The question this poses for us is how so many could possibly have failed for so long to see the problem we do about the words, how they could use them without either intellectual side-stepping or, as we might, seeking refuge in symbol and metaphor. What did they see about this that we somehow cannot, and what enabled them to do so? Further, would they, introduced to the intellectual acumen that we pride ourselves on as heirs of the Enlightenment and modern science, be able to agree with us?

---

3. Geertz, *Local Knowledge*, 275.

4. " . . . whoever eats this bread 'will not die forever'; for it is the body of Christ" (Ambrose, "The Mysteries," in *Theological and Dogmatic Works*, 22–23). In "The Sacraments" Ambrose made this even more explicit: "But that bread is bread before the words of the sacraments; when consecration has been added, from bread it becomes the flesh of Christ" (302).

Beyond the Body

Universes of Understanding

Let us for the moment accept the premise that too much separates us from the life and times of the early Church, not to mention from the person of the historical Jesus, for us to understand the words "this is" as they were either originally spoken or immediately understood. Attempts have been made, of course, and with considerable frequency in the ecumenical ambience of the Second Vatican Council (1962–65), to identify cultural features definitive of other historical periods that could serve as keys to unlock what otherwise seem unintelligible, and to some even unwise or deviant, dogmatic declarations. In 1968, for example, the Dominican theologian Edward Schillebeekx proposed that a clearer analysis of the proceedings of the Council of Trent (1545–63) would prove that the term transubstantiation, although representing the common intellectual understanding of those in attendance at the Council, stood only for how the matter could be put at the time, not for a dogmatic truth fulfilling the requirements of the Vincentian Canon: what always and everywhere and by everyone has been believed by the Church. Considering culturally idiosyncratic concepts essentially interchangeable so long as the basic belief of the faithful, in this case that Christ's body and blood are really present in the Eucharist, remains untouched, Schillebeeckx reviewed a range of for-the-time upstart, contemporary candidates to replace the no longer relevant transubstantiation. On the grounds that the concept of substance had not survived the onslaughts of twentieth-century science, a raft of new, more sacramentally oriented, terms was considered, among them transfunctionalization, transfinalization, and transsignification.[5] These were deemed safer possibilities than any potentially associated at that time with the wholesale anti-substantialism of Henri Bergson or the perspectival subjectivism of Maurice Merleau-Ponty.[6] Despite the impressive heft of the terms and their common emphasis on an accomplished change, however, they disappoint once we notice that far from embodying genuinely *avant garde* existentialist or other philosophical notions, each is in one form or another a transmogrification of the Aristotelian doctrine of formal and final causes as understood by Thomas Aquinas.[7] In short, the candidates to replace transubstantiation have more

---

5. Schillebeeckx, *Eucharist*, 108–9.

6. Ibid., 94.

7. See *ST* 1ae.2.3, where Aristotle's doctrine of the four causes supplies the structure for the arguments for the existence of God.

to do with the thirteenth than with either the sixteenth or the twentieth centuries, and the heralded new cross-culturally illuminating approach reveals itself in the end as unintentionally déjà vu. The barrier to resolving cultural impenetrability over time remains

But acknowledging the diachronicities of history and culture as insurmountable barriers to understanding need not entail hermeneutical suicide. That we cannot agree with or share the epistemological habits of another time or culture does not mean that we cannot know what those were or even recognize in them the workings of a logic not our own. This demands a tolerance rooted in modesty about the intellectual means our own age makes available to us, means that one day will likewise themselves recede diminishingly into history. It also requires that we reorient our expectation of the results from provable certainty to productive insight, to a methodology that both begins and ends with the disruptive, the "interesting."

Historians of both science and the visual arts have been particularly active in reassessments of the past that seek to view it on its own terms, conscientiously refusing to evaluate historic achievements as either halting steps toward the present or anticipations of modern categories of analysis. As a movement this began in the sciences, curiously enough with the same group of philosophers of a logical or mathematical bent who had championed the ideal of a unified science fulfilling nineteenth-century positivism's ambition for science to replace both religion and philosophy. In the arts attention increasingly turned to the conviction first voiced in anthropology and epitomized in Clifford Geertz's *Local Knowledge* that cultures could be understood only from within and on terms exclusively their own.

The history of science poses a unique opportunity to assess the growth, development, and replacement of systems of understanding that succeed each other owing to new, but essentially incompatible, foundational insights. The outlines of this process and its dynamics were first described in 1962 by T. S. Kuhn in what has become something of a durable classic on the subject, *The Structure of Scientific Revolutions*.[8] Kuhn recognized clearly

8. Kuhn, *Structure*. This was first published in 1962 as volume 2, number 2 of a monograph series collectively entitled the *International Encyclopedia of Unified Science*, led and advised by committees including Otto Neurath (Editor-in-Chief), Rudolf Carnap, Niels Bohr, John Dewey, Ernest Nagel, Bertrand Russell, and many similar figures of equal renown at the time. The work of this group built upon and continued that of the Vienna Circle of logical positivists of the early 1930s. Marilyn McCord Adams also sees in Kuhn's theory of scientific revolution an apt description of the transition from earlier theological Platonism to the thoroughgoing Aristotelianism of high scholasticism (Adams, *Some Later Medieval Theories*, 229–30).

that the basic data of the history of science simply would not support the sort of evolutionary, progressive narrative of interlocked efficient causes that characterized historical method at the time. Einsteinian mechanics, for instance, did not evolve from Newtonian mechanics in a continuity of development, but arose independently to challenge it, beginning from data Newton would not likely even have considered. To complicate matters further, Kuhn also noticed that sometimes new systems replaced old ones wholesale, but sometimes not, producing an unstable landscape of practical compromises acceptable only on the basis of the usefulness of their results.[9]

The central problem Kuhn faced, both as a scientist and an historian, was how the data, a congeries of seemingly irreconcilable systems of understanding, could be understood at all. This was a particularly crucial point, given that the series within which his book originated was dedicated without reservation to the idea of an uncompromising, and uncompromised, unity of the sciences. As model for a solution he reached not to philosophy, but to research in experimental psychology on perception, particularly on optical puzzles, including the Necker Cube, the Schröder Stairs, and a figure originated by University of Chicago psychologist Joseph Jastrow, the duck-rabbit.[10] Of these three, the Schröder Stairs, which present the viewer with either of two mutually exclusive senses of directional orientation, provided the most apt analogy for the differences between scientific systems. Both directional views were empirically verifiable, the gold standard for a positivist science. Each categorically excluded its alternate, since it was not possible to view both simultaneously. Kuhn concluded that differences between conflicting scientific systems must, like those of visually reversible figures, be created by mutually exclusive, governing directional "paradigms" that dictated their internal logic.[11] Such paradigms would succeed each other as discoveries of new data or unsolvable problems in existing data created "crises" for what had previously been considered "normal" science.[12] Changeovers like these Kuhn christened "paradigm shifts," minting an expression that would come to have broad application in almost every area of later twentieth-century culture.

Concurrently with Kuhn's work on paradigms, Wittgenstein had separately shown an interest in the oddity of reversible figures. For reasons of his

9. Kuhn, *Structure*, 72–74.
10. Images of these are readily available on the internet under these names.
11. Kuhn, *Structure*, 11–130.
12. Ibid., 66–76.

"This Is" and the Transience of Intelligibility

own less taken with perceptual problems like reversible stairs,[13] Wittgenstein concentrated on cases where language behavior, particularly naming, more precisely flagged the occurrence of a perceptual difference than descriptions of differing visual orientations could.[14] Refusing the enticement such problems offered to embark upon a discussion of ontology, he opted rather to treat such cases simply as instances of a linguistic phenomenon he dubbed "seeing-as," one possessed of its own internal logic in the form of a "language game."[15] This was quickly seized upon by some philosophers of religion as an analog for a religious faith that consisted primarily of a religious language use conscientiously stripped of any controversial ontological claims.[16]

Although treating religious faith exclusively in terms of "seeing-as" is fraught with both philosophical and religious difficulties,[17] this should not lead us to reject the concept wholesale. For one thing, while saying one sees a thing *as* something may not generally satisfy positivist empirical observation statement criteria, we still find it broadly used both effectively and intelligibly in ordinary language across a wide variety of situations. In regard to a real staircase we may, for example, see it as going up, going down, or just simply as being there. We may also see it, by which we mean "think of" it, as an opportunity for communication, an obstacle to communication, or an architectural achievement. All are meaningful descriptions not because of the staircase itself but because of the observer who makes them. No description, even the most rigidly empirical, could be meaningful if there were no one to make it. The proverbial tree that falls in the forest unobserved admits of no "independent" verification *or* falsi-

---

13. A statement that the Schröder Stairs appear reversible certainly qualifies as one of the irreducibly elementary empirical-description statements (Protokollsätze) of early logical positivism in its sometime form of logical "atomism." As such, it is simply not further describable. The famous concluding statement to the *Tractatus* to the effect that we ought to be quiet about what we cannot speak about ought rather to be taken as an avowal of this principle than as an invitation to mysticism (Wittgenstein, *Tractatus*, 150–51).

14. Ostensive definition, i.e., physical gestures like pointing, seem to provide the best means to communicate to someone else what the alternate views are of the latter.

15. Wittgenstein, *Philosophical Investigations*, 194.

16. Known popularly as "Wittgensteinian Fideism," this attracted numerous proponents, including John Hick and D. Z. Phillips (Hick, "Religious Faith," 20–35; Phillips, *Concept of Prayer*).

17. See, for example, Heaney, "Faith," 189–98. For the contemporary state of this very long-lived debate, see Nielsen and Phillips, *Wittgensteinian Fideism?*

fication, without which it amounts to little more than an epistemic myth. Uses of seeing-as that are more generalized than observation statements serve very useful functions in broader argument and analysis, particularly as syncategorematic movers of discussion to consider alternative data or presuppositions.

Kuhn's concepts of paradigm and paradigm shift offer us what is in effect an algorithm for understanding historically and culturally bound intellectual systems that differ markedly from our own, even to the point of unintelligibility. They also explain in great measure how those systems rise to cultural dominance and are then replaced by later, incompatible, developments. They uncover aspects of alternate systems that may have a validity in their own right that time and distance deny us in the present. As kin to the more generalized instances of seeing-as mentioned above, they offer us a language in which to discuss the otherwise undiscussable, with an eye to results that may both raise and answer different questions from those with which we began.

Two Paradigms

Of the five senses, two, sight and hearing, are the primary vehicles in Western thought for modeling human knowledge and its acquisition. We hear words as sounds, as individual semantic or semiotic units, and we say that we "see" their meaning. We can call sight and hearing "models" on the grounds that they supply much of our language about how we come to know things, and "paradigms" in that they also provide rules for how that language is used.[18] We cannot "see" our seeing or "hear" our hearing, nor can we simultaneously "understand" our own understanding.[19] But we can talk intelligibly about these in terms related to vision and hearing, terms whose use is quite familiar and unexceptional to us. If these be language games, we know how to play them.

When we take sight as a model for knowledge and understanding, we do so because we find in it a primitive, irreducible experience untroubled by ambiguities.[20] We either see, or we do not, with only a token concession, in remarks about rose-colored glasses, to the possibilities of nuance.

---

18. Thus Kuhn on the function of paradigms in providing criteria for and rules of procedure (*Structure*, 35–42).

19. Cf. Aristotle, *On the Soul* 417a.

20. "... the perception of proper objects is always true" (ibid., 427 b13).

"This Is" and the Transience of Intelligibility

Like any model, sight also has limits that are commonly understood and accepted, e.g., that sight and understanding are neither identical to each other nor necessary and sufficient conditions for each other are matters of practical experience. The transparency of the relationship between sight, understanding, and the language of sight harbors no hidden difficulties. Or so it would seem.

A recognition that historically there have, however, been two very different and essentially incompatible, theories of vision, and that these have had broad formative, paradigmatic, influence on scientific, philosophical, and artistic culture, appeared first among historians of science.[21] The earliest of the two theories was that of Plato, for whom vision was a spontaneous activity of both the eye and the soul which, through an invisible physical ray of vision lighted up the object to be seen:

> And so in the vessel of the head, they first of all put a face in which they inserted organs to minister in all things to the providence of the soul, and they appointed this part, which has authority, to be the natural front. And of the organs they first contrived the eyes to give light, and the principle according to which they were inserted was as follows. So much of fire as would not burn, but gave a gentle light, they formed into a substance akin to the light of everyday life, and the pure fire which is within us and related thereto they made to flow through the eyes in a stream smooth and dense, compressing the whole eye and especially the center part, so that it kept out everything of a coarser nature and allowed to pass only this pure element. When the light of day surrounds the stream of vision, then like falls upon like, and they coalesce, and one body is formed by natural affinity in the line of vision, wherever the light that falls from within meets an external object.[22]

This theory was, however, flatly rejected by Aristotle, for very commonsense reasons that would inform work on the science of optics over the next millennium and a half:

> ... if the eye were actually fire, as Empedocles says, and as is stated in the *Timaeus,* (45c) and if vision occurred when light issues from the eye as from a lantern, why should not vision be equally possible in the dark? It is quite futile to say, as the *Timaeus* (45d) does, that on its emergence from the eye it is extinguished in the dark; for what meaning can we attach to this extinguishing of light?

21 Lindberg, *Theories of Vision* and *Beginnings.*
22. Plato, *Timaeus* 45a–c in *Collected Dialogues of Plato.*

Beyond the Body

> In general it is unreasonable to suppose that seeing occurs by something issuing from the eye; that the ray of vision reaches as far as the stars, or goes to a certain point and coalesces with the object, as some think. It would be better to suppose that coalescence occurs in the very heart of the eye.... Consequently the part within must be transparent and receptive of light.[23]

Aristotle's view of perception emphasized the passivity of sense experience: "Sensation consists, ... in being moved and acted upon; for it is held to be [a] sort of change of state,"[24] and "Vision occurs when the sensitive faculty is acted upon."[25] Further, "The visible, then, is colour, *i.e.*, that which overlies what is in itself visible; by 'in itself' we mean not that the object is by its definition visible but that it has within itself the cause of its visibility."[26]

The first of these theories of vision, that of Plato and his later followers, has now come to be known as "extramissive," owing to its reliance upon an emanation or radiation *from* the physical eye. That of Aristotle, emphasizing as it does the primacy of the object in reflecting rays that must enter *into* the eye from without in order for vision to occur, is correspondingly termed "intromissive."[27] Quite aside from any physical differences involved, these represent very different and basically incompatible paradigms of knowledge and understanding. The extramissive paradigm, parent of later idealisms, puts the mind foremost in determining what its experiences are experiences *of*. Its criteria for such judgments are abstract concepts, the ideas, that the necessarily eternal soul brings to its present life from a previous immaterial existence. Things are, and are *as*, what the soul, through the activity of its eyes, determines them to be. They are, properly speaking, *objects* of seeing, their reality in effect created in the act of seeing itself. Limits to the process are set by the incommensurability of the ideal and the eternal with the physical and the transient, a chasm that even the simple arithmetic of counting cannot in principle bridge with an accurate account.[28] The world is what we see there, accurately so to the extent that our reach is matched by our grasp, as it were.

---

23. Aristotle, "On Sense and Sensible Objects," 437b, 438a–b in Aristotle, *On the Soul, Parva Naturalia, On Breath*, 207–83.

24. Aristotle, *On the Soul* 416 b 35.

25. Ibid., 419 a 17–18.

26. Ibid., 418 a 29–31.

27. Lindberg, *Beginnings*, 314–15.

28. Plato, *Theaetetus* 204b–205b in *Collected Dialogues of Plato*.

"This Is" and the Transience of Intelligibility

The intromissive paradigm, on the other hand, begins from a world of objects that exist in their own right, independently of anyone perceiving them. They come to be and pass away courtesy of laws of causality that, like them, the perceiving subject can learn or deduce from experience. By simple association the commonalities among them come to be named by general terms that can be more broadly applied. True knowledge occurs when what the knower sees is what is there, a criterion that medieval Aristotelians would enshrine in the expression *adequatio intellectus ad rem*, the correct alignment of the intellect with the thing. Knowledge occurs passively, and it grows primarily by increasing the mass of experience to which the knower is exposed.

The cultural and historical positioning of both these paradigms is nothing if not "interesting." Despite the fact that the intromissive theory, albeit in a modern form, is firmly ensconced in what for us is "normal" science, its extramissive opposite features at least as much, if not more, in everyday language, including that familiar from biblical sources. The eye, for instance, is the "organ of sight," possessing "the power of vision," the blind being those who have "lost the power of sight." It is the eye that carries on that activity by which we apprehend or perceive something, by which we "exercise the faculty of vision." We "keep our eye on" something, having it "under our gaze," until it is "out of sight" or out of our "range of vision." We "see to it" that something is done, and we cast an "angry eye" should the result not be what we were "looking for."[29] In the New Testament "the eye is the lamp of the body" (Mt 6:22), and if its activities cause us moral difficulties, we should "throw it away" (Mt 18:9). Those activities can be blocked or impeded by either our own failure to use our eyes properly (Mk 8:18, Acts 28:27), by some external agency that hampers their function (Lk 24:16), or by simply physical, although still extraordinary means, like the scales that fell from Paul's eyes (Acts 9:18). God also sees, gazes: "all are naked and laid bare to the eyes of the one to whom we must render an account" (Heb 4:13), whose "eyes are like a flame of fire" (Rev 19:12).

As a paradigm for knowledge, the extramissive theory propounded by Plato in the *Timaeus* finds perhaps its most apt corollary in the Myth of the Cave in *Republic* X (514a–517a), where the only realities available to the captives are shadows of things and echoes of voices. One of the prisoners escapes and sees first the deception being played and then, after much effort, the world outside the cave, where objects can be seen as they really

---

29. Cf. *Oxford English Dictionary*, 2nd ed., s.v. "eye," "sight," and "vision."

are owing to the light of the sun. Should the captive attempt, however, to return below with the good news of his discoveries, he would not only be disbelieved, but would likely be threatened with death for his opinions. What the myth establishes through description is a reality existing in distinct ontological tiers, as it were, the very least of which is the only one that is most immediately available to us. The captives see shadows, but these are still images of actual things, however limited. The same objects could also be seen directly, although imperfectly, within the conditions of the cave, and more perfectly still in sunlight. The restrictions on seeing are caused not by the eye itself but by the availability of light with which to see.

The active role of the eye in both physical vision and intellectual understanding formed an integral part of the Platonic tradition across a broad spectrum of Greco-Roman culture. In the first century of our era, for instance, Philo Judaeus described vision in just such activist terms:

> . . . but the energies of the eyes when they are open are continuous and uninterrupted, as the eyes are never satisfied or wearied, but continue to operate in accordance with the connection which they have with the soul.[30]

The epitome of such activity takes place when the eyes, with the help of intellectual light, rise from viewing the ordinary objects of sense to the contemplation of the heavens, which themselves are signs of the highest, intellectual realities.[31] The remark of Paul that "for now we see in a mirror, dimly, but then we will see face to face" (1 Cor 13:12) likewise depends upon a contrast between what it is possible to see under present circumstance and what the unfettered vision would be capable of. Again, vision itself is not at fault here, but only the conditions under which it is exercised.

As the literature that would later constitute the canonical New Testament came gradually to be regarded as Scripture, with the public status that this entailed, the conviction that "mere" words were in some manner part of higher realities became a constant of exegetical method. Origen, for instance, in his great *Commentary on John* makes frequent mention of the "mystical" sense of words and puts the mystical or anagogical on a par with the allegorical as a method of interpretation.

The most historically influential proponent of this view, whose casting of it would shape Western exegesis even in the Reformation, was

---

30. Philo Judaeus, "On Abraham," in *The Essential Philo*, 19.
31. Philo Judaeus, "On the Creation of the World," in *The Essential Philo*, 17–18.

"This Is" and the Transience of Intelligibility

Augustine. Throughout his life and long career, he remained intrigued by the problems presented to both common sense and the science of his times by the Genesis account of creation. Then, as now, a literal reading of that account revealed logical inconsistencies in the progress of the narrative and raised semantic questions about what appeared at first to be the simple, straightforward meaning of terms like "light," "day," and "said." Since passive perception can see only what is immediately before it, vision, and its intellectual counterpart, the understanding, must necessarily be active if any higher, incontrovertible, sense of these terms is to be attained. Predictably, thus, in *The Literal Meaning of Genesis* Augustine subscribes explicitly to the extramissive theory of vision: "The shaft of rays from our eyes, to be sure, is a shaft of light," although he tempers this with the provision that some external light may also be necessary for seeing in certain situations.[32] He further subscribes to a trio of levels of understanding, including corporeal, spiritual, and intellectual, that correspond to three successively more excellent kinds of vision.[33] Quite contrary to what one might expect from its title, the work begins with the unblushing declaration that "No Christian will dare say that the narrative must not be taken in a figurative sense."[34] From this beginning Augustine goes on to conclude that the literal or "historical" sense of "light" is intellectual light, of "day" a period of time with no determinable limits, and of "said" as in "God said" no communicative utterance in any human language.[35] The literal or historical sense is, quite obviously, not the corporeal at all, but something much higher.

Contrasting Ontologies

The independence that characterizes physical objects as objects of vision in the *intromissive* paradigm has important consequences for how those are known. An object seen remains and remains *as* it is even if we are not looking at it. It has its own existence and is what it is based on the principle

---

32. Augustine, *Genesis* 1.16. Augustine's point was that before daylight per se was created on the fourth day vision would have been possible only to the extent that the amount of light resident within the eye itself could allow for that. In *On the Trinity* 9.4.3 he similarly describes vision as an active process, although further on in Book Eleven (11.2.2) more allowance seems to be made for the independence and integrity of identity of objects characteristic of an intromissive theory of vision.

33. Augustine, *Genesis* 11.22.

34. Ibid., 1.1.

35. Ibid., 1.17.34–35; 4.1.1; 1.2.4–6.

of identity, i.e., that it cannot be and not be the same thing, in the same way, at the same time. Referring language use is restrained by this in terms of the level of referential complexity that is open to it. Objects are discrete individuals that cannot be said to be each other in any literal way. Any attempt to do so, therefore, can only be carried out using some commonly acceptable form of words, in effect a language game, that fulfills a purpose other than direct reference. For Aristotle and the literary tradition that follows him, metaphor is that form of words, characterized as a literary device: "the application of an alien name by transference either from genus to species, or from species to genus, or from species, or by analogy, that is, proportion."[36] The purpose of metaphor is not reference, but persuasion, beauty, style, what the author known as Longinus would later call "the sublime."[37] The allowance of metaphor, as noted earlier, expands what can be said of an object beyond what is possible by direct reference. It does so, however, at the expense of identity.

Instances of "seeing-as" fall variously within the bounds and restraints of metaphor. To see something *as* something else carries with it the proviso that it still is not in fact that other thing. Visual examples of seeing-as must fulfill the criteria of the law of identity, albeit in different ways: the Schröder Stairs can be seen differently, but not in the same way or at the same time. Less hard-edged examples like seeing stairs as means of communication or, conversely, as obstacles to communication, fare better in terms of simultaneous recognition, but at the expense of objective reference. One unfortunate casualty of this, of course, is that to say we see the Eucharist *as* the body of Christ is to say as well that it really is not. Seeing-as, as understood to operate under the intromissive paradigm of vision, cannot solve our difficulties over the intelligibility of "this is."

The extramissive paradigm for vision and knowledge endures in our own time primarily in a fringe of idiomatic usage that has little, if any, impact on how we manage the world. The ubiquity of acceptance for a passive model of perception in fact renders unwelcome any hint of an intellect as aggressively active as extramissive vision requires. Thinking one's perception of things superior to the reality of those things raises suspicions of egotism, conceit, and denial in the face of "facts." Both the foundational ego of Descartes and the transcendental ego of Kant have been summarily

---

36. Aristotle, *Theory of Poetry* 1457b4–5. This emphasis on the transference of names in metaphor appears as well in Aristotle, *Rhetoric* 1404b–1405b.

37. Longinus, "On the Sublime," 121, 140–42.

replaced by the complex, fractured identities of postmodern life first introduced by Freud. The philosophical idealism of the extramissive paradigm must of necessity seem to us little more than epistemic narcissism.

The intellectual structure of extramissive perception and understanding, however, depends not upon the qualities of transient objects external to sense, but upon concepts necessarily greater than those because of, at the very least, their broader applicability. Any comparison of passing existences to intellectual categories finds the latter both more flexible in principle and more enduring than the former as well. The recognition that this is so, not simply a judgment that this is so, supports the added intimation that to persevere actively over time across a broad range of circumstances is to exist both more and more fully than is possible for even the most adamantine of objects. And where judgments are to be made, it will be on the basis of whatever is most certain and enduring, those concepts the mind takes with it to the viewing of reality and the objects it sees there with their help.[38] Rather than the logic of an observer seeing an object *A as* [identical to] another object *B*, even though it is not, the genuinely active intellect and vision of the observer sees *A* as an instance of *B*, where the latter is an object or concept of greater applicability and/or durability than *A*. The criteria of judgment are based not on observable qualities or accidents but on what the intellect, through the eyes, actively sees there. What can be seen of the object passively must, in such a situation, be far less convincing or important than what can be seen actively.

One additional corollary of the extramissive vision paradigm ought not to be overlooked. Physical objects considered *intro*missively are possessed of a separate and distinct existence that is not, as it were, shared with other similar objects. The concept of metaphor provides the only, and a rhetorical, means to bridge that divide, and that at best only provisionally. Objects of *extra*missive vision and understanding, on the other hand, seem to enjoy a continuity, rather than a contiguity, of existence. In Augustine's reading of Genesis, for instance, days in the creation, although not identical to the days we know, are still days, as are light, voice, and so on. "Being," in short, is not parceled out piecemeal in distinct objects but shared across reality, both physical and conceptual. It is this "univocity of being," a not

---

38. This form of Platonism is thankfully not without its modern proponents, particularly in the scientific community. The twentieth-century mathematician Kurt Gödel, for instance, has often been quoted for his remarks on a mathematical intuition of sets that is remarkably like a perception of them as real objects. Referenced in Polkinghorne, *Belief in God*, 129.

uncontroversial notion, that makes possible seeing in objects more than is possible for purely passive viewing.

Identifying the differences that a paradigm of knowledge based on an extramissive theory of vision makes possible provides some glimpse into how statements that seem outrageous or unintelligible to us now might not always have seemed so. The thoughts of Jesus in saying "this is" are still unavailable to us, but the manner of thinking of those who later read those words or heard them spoken in the liturgy perhaps less so. Early Western medieval debates about which body of Jesus, the historical earthly or the post-Resurrection heavenly, was present in the Eucharist point to an understanding of an ontological continuity between the visible and invisible that is part of a way of thought rather than simply a muscular exercise of belief construed as an incomplete form of knowledge.

The Anatomy of a Shift

Paradigm changes of the sort described by Kuhn play an obvious and significant part in the history of Eucharistic doctrine in the Western Church. The absence of interest in formal ontological questions of reference about the Eucharist in the early centuries is certainly in harmony with the predominantly neoplatonic predilections of figures like Clement of Alexandria and Origen. Despite his seemingly unequivocal remarks equating the Eucharist with the historical body of Christ,[39] remarks that would later serve as a benchmark for controversies in the Carolingian ninth century, Ambrose seems to have had little effect in ameliorating the platonism of his most important protégé, Augustine. But the differences in their respective positions would fuel those later controversies and set in motion the rise of the more physical understanding of the Eucharist ultimately sanctioned by the Fourth Lateran Council of 1215 and by the Council of Trent in endorsing the term "transubstantiation" for general use. Those endorsements both embodied and completed, over a span of time roughly from the ninth to the sixteenth centuries, an irreversible shift from one major paradigm of knowledge to another. It would terminate in a fully-articulated system of thought in harmony with an intromissive paradigm of vision and knowledge, unfortunately a system of thought no less stubbornly unintelligible outside its own frame of reference than its predecessor had been.

---

39. See n. 4 above.

"This Is" and the Transience of Intelligibility

The formative Eucharistic controversy of the ninth-century West was prompted by a treatise, the first ever solely on that topic, by Paschasius Radbertus of the abbey of Corbie. Written in 831, *On the Body and Blood of the Lord* was intended originally for internal use in the monastery school.[40] In 843 a revised version was submitted to king Charles the Bald, who apparently requested a critical assessment of the question from Radbertus' monastic colleague Ratramnus. That some contention must have surrounded the issue seems clear, if only owing to Ratramnus's position as one of the foremost controversialists of the times.[41] His response, of the same title, provides an admirably constructed alternate view of the matter, as well as an opportunity to gauge the scholarly acuity of an age intellectually very remote from our own.[42]

History has dealt quite ambiguously with both these protagonists and with their works, owing to some degree to history's inability to do without an overarching narrative to arbitrate, or in some cases even create, what constitutes the past. For the tradition that began with the Reformation, Radbertus's treatise marked the apex of the slippery slope to a degraded Christianity, one doctrinally chained to superstition by a church that had made transubstantiation an article of faith. Ratramnus, on this view, stands out as a pre-Calvinist hero who kept the heritage of Augustine faithfully and stood foursquare against religious primitivism and the forces of superstition. Roman Catholics, for their part, reckon Radbertus to have sowed the seeds, in an intuitively correct but theologically unsophisticated way, of the most central religious doctrine of that Church. For some his well-meaning but limited efforts elicit only faint, grudging praise. Others would rather ignore him altogether.[43] Thankfully, the strongest Catholic historical scholarship has taken this in hand by exploring in great depth and sensitivity not only the doctrinal, but particularly the liturgical context of the Frankish church for his work, painting a far more complete picture

---

40. Paschasius Radbertus, *De corpore*, vii.

41. See Wallace-Hadrill, *Frankish Church*, 362–66, and Pelikan, *Christian Tradition*, 1:80–88.

42. The most textually detailed account of this controversy to date, and one which sheds a great deal of light of Radbertus's creativity as a theologian is that of David Ganz. Of particular interest is his analysis of the patristic sources of the opposing arguments (*Corbie*, 81–102).

43. See, for example, Joseph M. Powers, who skips from Amalarius of Metz to Berengar of Tours with no mention of either Radbertus or Ratramnus (Powers, *Eucharistic Theology*, 27–28).

of Carolingian religion than was ever before possible.[44] Forging interpretive relationships through comparison of texts can, however, tend to have a leveling effect, concentrating as it does on sameness rather than difference, reinforcement rather than anomaly. Without in any way faulting the mass of scholarship to date that has revealed so much about the historical emergence of transubstantiation as a doctrinal term,[45] reading the concept of a paradigm shift onto that history does enable us to assess it rather differently, certainly more holistically. The result, predictably, is not an alternative developmental narrative, but a series of observations that collectively suggest what might better be thought of as a picture than an interpretation. There are four areas to address: the historical outline of the shift involved, the philosophical climate in which it occurred, the hermeneutical point on which it revolved, and the new significance of miracles as data for theological speculation.

A Historical Frame

Setting aside for the moment development or progress as standards of interpretation, it is difficult to avoid noticing a number of similarities that effectively *frame* the period of time from the controversy of Radbertus and Ratramnus to the Council of Trent. One quite obvious one is the physicality of Radbertus' conception of the Eucharist as the body of Christ, notwithstanding the invisibility of that condition. Perhaps almost as striking is the force of his declaration at the outset, "It is . . . clear that nothing is possible outside the will of God or contrary to it, but all things wholly yield to him,"[46] words that do not simply "prefigure" but certainly express the same sentiments as those with which William of Ockham some half a millennium later distinguished the absolute power of God (*de potentia absoluta*) from the action of God in creation (*de potentia ordinata*) in his *de sacramento altaris*.[47] Medievalists have not failed to notice the continuity on into the

---

44. Special note needs to be made here of the pioneering work of Henri de Lubac in *Corpus Mysticum*.

45. The most complete treatments of this remain Geiselmann, *Eucharistielehre* and Jorissen, *Entfaltung*. For a very different but equally authoritative perspective, see Stock, *Implications of Literacy*, 241–325.

46. Pascasius Radbertus, "The Lord's Body and Blood," 94; idem, *De corpore et sanguine*, 13.

47. William of Ockham, *De Sacramento*, 110–17. For further detail see Oberman, *Harvest*, 30–56.

"This Is" and the Transience of Intelligibility

fifteenth century of Eucharistic miracle as an integral part of the medieval experience,[48] a linkage that Radbertus was the first to address in a systematic fashion. It was one of these same miracles that Aquinas would later feel a need to deal with temporizingly in the *Summa Theologica*.[49] Curiously, however, there is one aspect of this frame owing entirely to Ratramnus, specifically his insistence that adopting a physicalist rather than a figurative view of the Eucharist would require that some account be given of the *change* that must necessarily take place in the bread and wine.[50]

Together Radbertus and Ratramnus are paradigmatic for the course of theological thinking that follows. That the more physical views of the former prevail, despite the general disapproval of them by major contemporary figures,[51] certainly speaks to their perceived difference from what was then the established theological norm. That they would replace that norm over the coming centuries is the basis of the suggestion that a shift in paradigms of knowledge did indeed occur. Perhaps nothing is more emblematic of such a shift than the fate of the contestants. The Catholic Church celebrates the feast of *Saint* Paschasius Radbertus on April 26. Ratramnus's work, despite its seeming favor at the time, would live in ignominy until being removed only in 1900 from the *Index of Forbidden Books*.

Inherent Ambiguities

The existence of rival, contradictory assessments of these two ninth-century figures derives not only from later theological bias but also from a generic ambiguity, characteristic of their age, that needs to be more pointedly recognized. For one thing, the physicality of Radbertus and the Augustinian neoplatonism of Ratramnus may have stood in much less stark contrast to them than to us, for whom the rediscovered Aristotle of the twelfth and thirteenth and the reclaimed Plato of the fourteenth centuries were indeed mutually opposed. The Carolingian age inherited its philosophical underpinnings rather from Boethius, whose avowed aim had been to promote

---

48. Miri Rubin in particular shows how miracles were utilized for teaching purposes (*Corpus Christi*, 108–28).

49. *ST* 3a.76.8.

50. Ratramnus of Corbie, "Christ's Body and Blood," 122–23; idem, *Ratramnus de corpore et sanguine*, xiv–xv, 37.

51. Rabanus Maurus in particular (Ratramnus of Corbie, *Ratramnus de corpore et sanguine*, 5).

Beyond the Body

not a difference but a harmony of the thought of Plato and Aristotle.[52] This was attested particularly by his translation into Latin of a supposed work of the latter, the *Isagoge,* actually by the Neoplatonist Porphyry. Of Plato the ninth century knew only the *Timaeus*. Of Aristotle it knew only some of the logic, specifically the *Categories,* wherein "substance" is treated not as the metaphysical entity it became in the later Aristotle of the *Physics* and the *Metaphysics,* but as a characteristic aspect of experience.[53] *Substantia* does indeed appear in the texts of both Radbertus and Ratramnus, but in a usage innocent of both metaphysics and the passion for philosophical precision that centuries later would become de rigueur owing to Peter Abelard.[54] The same disregard for or lack of interest in unearthing philosophically contradictory positions also colored their appropriation of the wide range of grammatical works of both Stoic and Arisotelian provenance then available to them.[55]

A more specific ambiguity arises when we contrast what we can know of the character and position of each author. In Radbertus we have a dedicated educator and biblical expositor whose scriptural commentaries would remain authoritative for several centuries.[56] His initial presentation of the treatise to his abbot begins playfully with an acrostic on his own name and monastic status,[57] situating the text to follow not as a contribution to philosophical debate but as a literary and exegetical effort strongly marked by the theory-laden grammatical preoccupations of the Carolingian educational reform.[58] But although theoretical grammar and exegesis supply the

---

52. Pelikan, *Christian Tradition*, 1:42.

53. Kneale and Kneale, *Development*, 25–32.

54. On substance as a category, see Luhtala, "Syntax and Dialectic," 151–54.

55. This was particularly true of the concept of *vox* or voice that would eventually provide the basis for questions about the meaning of universal terms (Irvine, *Textual Culture*, 95).

56. In the time of Hugh of St. Victor, nearly three centuries later, Radbertus's literal commentary on the book of Lamentations would still be the standard (Smalley, *Study of the Bible*, 102).

57. The initial letters of each line collectively spell out RADBERTUSLEVITA (Pascasius Radbertus, *De corpore et sanguine*, 1). Some of the best known personages of the time, including both Alcuin and Hrabanus Maurus, also composed acrostics, which had been fashionable among educators and expositors for at least a century. See Law, *Grammar and Grammarians*, 231–32.

58. Foremost in this was interest, prompted particularly by Alcuin, in the philosophical issues raised by those sections of Priscian's grammar that dealt with the referential status of pronouns (Law, *Grammar and Grammarians*, 136–37). As it happens,

method of his treatise, Radbertus is careful to provide a pledge of fidelity to the most authoritative sources, listing for his abbot's reassurance Cyprian, Ambrose, Augustine, Jerome, Hilary of Poitiers, Isidore of Seville, Gregory, and Bede, who had, among all his many works, authored a Latin grammar. Radbertus repeats these assurances in his preface to the king, along with the obligatory deprecatory references to his own humble status.

Ratramnus, also a monk of Corbie, enters the scene by royal order, not to refute the views of Radbertus, whom he never mentions, but to explain his own. The royal request for clarification focuses on two points. One is whether the body and blood of Christ is in the Eucharist only *figuratively* or whether it is there in *truth*, which latter expression we may with only slight differences in nuance take to mean what we understand as *factually*. At stake in this distinction is the guarantee that the Eucharist is neither mystically nor metaphorically the body of Christ but "that body, which was born of Mary, suffered, died, and was buried."[59] Where Radbertus turns to scripture for both support and concept, Ratramnus argues a case founded heavily upon fidelity to patristic sources, including Cyril of Jerusalem, Ambrose, Augustine, Isidore, Jerome, and Fulgentius of Ruspe. Radbertus will in fact turn explicitly to these sources only in retrospect when, in later years, he includes them as an appendix in a letter to his former monastic colleague Fredugard.[60] Further, where Ratramnus will use sacrament and sacramental action as models, with baptism his primary example, Radbertus makes a more powerful, if theologically riskier, appeal to the Incarnation as paradigm.

Truth and Figure

The theoretical point on which Radbertus and Ratramnus appear to divide is their differing understandings of the terms *figura* and *veritas*. For Ratramnus, steeped in an Augustinian tradition deeply committed to the

---

a manuscript of Priscian's *Institutio de nomine et pronomine et verbo* is traceable to the library at Corbie in Radbertus's time (Passalacqua, "Priscian's Institutio," 195–96). As Martin Irvine notes, "the library of Corbie, to judge from surviving manuscripts and its twelfth-century catalogue, also had one of the most complete collections of grammatical *artes* and classical and Christian *auctores* on the continent" (*Textual Culture*, 342).

59. Ratramnus, "Christ's Body and Blood," 119. In full, "utrum ipsum corpus sit quod de Maria natum est et passum mortuum et sepultum quodque resurgens et caelos ascendens ad dexteram patris consideat" (idem, *Ratramnus de corpore et sanguine*, 24).

60. Pascasius Radbertus, *De corpore et sanguine*, 162–73.

extramissive theory of vision,[61] the figural sense of a text is always its higher, truer meaning. *Veritas*, on the other hand, is reserved for plain facts that may occasion higher meanings but of themselves do not possess them. For the body of Christ to exist physically in the Eucharist as a fact would both demean it and obviate either the necessity or the opportunity for faith.[62] The Eucharist is food for the soul; its relation to mundane nourishment is immaterial.

In contrast to the polished courtliness and scholarly demeanor of Ratramnus's treatise, Radbertus's position is deceptively simple. Both the proximity of grammar to dialectic in the *trivium* of the early medieval curriculum and contemporary interest in the philosophical implications of grammar that had been raised by the Byzantine grammarian Priscian show to advantage in his analysis of language, particularly written language:

> ... through characters or the figures of letters we as small children first progressed gradually to reading, later to the spiritual senses and understanding of the Scriptures. ... What else are the figures of letters than their characters, that through them force and power and utterance of spirit are demonstrated to the eyes? ... Yet the characters of the letters are not falsity, nor are they anything but letters. ... He has left us in this sacrament a visible figure and character of flesh and blood, so that through them our soul and our flesh are richly nourished for grasping things invisible and spiritual by faith.[63]

Although there seems to be less difference than expected between this view of *figura* and that of Ratramnus in that both ultimately defer to a higher reality, Radbertus here chooses to ally *figura* not with literary trope but with the visible form or character of the letters of the alphabet. These are what they visibly are, marks on paper, but with no sense that they are lessened in any way by their conventional materiality. Neither are they

---

61. As in Augustine, *Genesis*, I.16. Unfortunately, it does not appear that either Radbertus or Ratramnus knew of this work, and particularly of its much more pointed discussion of literal meaning than is found in Augustine "On Christian Doctrine," 24ff. (Ratramnus of Corbie, "Christ's Body and Blood," 120–21; idem, *Ratramnus de corpore et sanguine*, x, 35).

62. "For, if as some would have it, nothing is here received figuratively, but everything is visible in truth, faith does not operate here, since nothing spiritual takes place, but whatever it is, it is wholly received according to its bodily sense" (Ratramnus, "Christ's Body and Blood," 119; idem, *Ratramnus de corpore et sanguine*, xxxiii, 42).

63. Pascasius Radbertus, "The Lord's Body and Blood," 103.

simply occasions for the eye to bring the force of the mind to bear upon them while seeking ideal types with which to compare them. The Augustinian doctrine of language as sign is here transformed into a sacramental understanding of writing, and reading, where words have become the loci of spiritual conveyance, *through* which, rather than by means of which, access to higher understanding is possible. Because of this capacity the text, both in its constituent words and in itself as a whole, has an individually distinct ontological value.

This understanding of writing accords well with the grammatical thinking of the time, most notably in the concept of reading with the *oculis mentis*, the eye of the mind, proposed a century earlier by the grammarian Vergilius Maro Grammaticus.[64] The concept of "seeing-through" conjoins physical object and meaning in an act of understanding such that each retains its individual identity in a way not possible when one of two objects is seen-as the other. How formative of Eucharistic belief the notion of "seeing-through" would prove to be is very much evidenced in the later medieval liturgical and artistic phenomenon of the "Gregory Mass" described by Carolyn Bynum.[65] This began from the legend, known in Radbertus's time, of Gregory the Great seeing the suffering Savior, the Man of Sorrows, behind the physical setting of the Eucharistic action in the Mass, illustrating, exemplifying, and guaranteeing its saving effect. More than simply a convenient theme for altar pieces, the Gregory Mass visually demonstrates a mechanics of Eucharistic presence first suggested by Radbertus, one that would model both piety and practice, though seemingly not theological language, throughout the Middle Ages and up into the Reformation.

Implied in "seeing-through" is a very different notion of what is called "substance." As a category of experience, rather than as a representation of the source or locus of an act of *being*, substance for Carolingian thinkers like Radbertus and Ratramnus functions within everyday language and grammar as the subject of qualities and the grammatical subject or agent and, *pari passu*, object, of action.[66] The structural implications of such a subject/verb configuration of verbal reasoning go some distance in illuminating the differences between the two positions. For Radbertus, using the hypostatic union of the Incarnation as model for the identity of the Eucharistic elements with the physical body of Christ, the Eucharist cannot

---

64. Law, *Grammar and Grammarians*, 223–45.

65. Bynum, "Seeing and Seeing Beyond," 208–40.

66. Luhtala, "Syntax and Dialectic," 150–61.

be the object result of any action that would have effected change but must itself stand as subject and, potentially, as agent. It should not be overlooked that this description of Eucharistic presence is one that directly implies personal, rather than simply bodily, identity with the historical Jesus. In the artistic expression of the Gregory Mass, it is not the consecrated host that saves, but the Christ whom it enables us to see through it. Ratramnus, on the other hand, having used baptism as a before-and-after model of sacramental change, is bound to consider the Eucharist grammatically as the resultant *object* of liturgical, sacramental action. Having the sacramental system as paradigm and priority forces him to insist on there being a change, even though "one must not inquire by what method this could be done, but exercise faith that it was done."[67]

It is primarily Ratramnus's insistence on the necessity to explain change, not Radbertus's implication of personal identity, that would shape the technical discussion of the centuries to follow, sparked particularly by the ill-fated resurrection of Ratramnus's notion of Eucharist as figure in the Berengarian controversy of the eleventh century. That technical discussion would at last find its proper métier with the recovery in the twelfth century of the later, more powerfully developed, views on substance of Aristotle's *Physics* and *Metaphysics*. These would sort well with and serve to enhance a physical understanding of Eucharistic change. The high scholastic doctrine of the soul as substantial form of the body, however, would leave largely untouched those aspects of Eucharistic piety that sought union with the person of Christ in the sacrament, rather than a spiritual "nourishment."

The Impact of Miracles

Both Protestant and Catholic history alike have looked askance at the Eucharistic miracles recounted by Radbertus. For the former they constituted an unsubtle means of control over an uneducated populace by a church that treasured its own authority over that of the gospel. For the latter they were an unpleasant reminder of the constant threat that unschooled religious fervor posed for the maintenance of orthodox belief and, correspondingly, civil/ecclesiastical order. In an age when what were once miracles are now routinely performed in laboratories, it is likewise difficult for us to share

---

67. Ratramnus, "Christ's Body and Blood," 125; idem, *Ratramnus de corpore et sanguine*, xxv, 40.

Radbertus's enthusiasm for the phenomena he recounts. It is difficult to tell whether their never being mentioned by Ratramnus meant that he, like us, thought them unworthy of consideration or that they constituted a third rail of customary piety he dared not touch.

Miracles, regardless of what we may think of them, still certainly fulfill the requirements of the "interesting." Except for any accidental similarities to each other, they invariably represent the invasion of "normal" reality by forces or events that are alien, uncontrollable, "other," or just simply very different from the anticipated, in short, an intervention. For a paradigm of knowledge based on an extramissive theory of vision, the probity of unusual events like miracles and visions is founded not on what is given to sight but on the state of mind or spiritual wellbeing of the one doing the seeing. Thus Augustine on distinguishing between hallucinations and genuine visionary experiences:

> But it sometimes happens that by too much mental concentration, or due to some illness (as sometimes happens to those delirious with fever), or by the action of some spirit, good or bad, images of corporeal things are produced in the spirit in such a way that they are presented to the corporeal senses as if they were bodies, although we still remain attentive in our senses. In this way we see what are images of body in the spirit. . . . But when the soul's intention is completely turned away or snatched away from the body's senses, then it is more usually called ecstasy. . . . The soul's entire gaze is directed to images of bodies in its spiritual power, or through its intellectual power toward incorporeal things without any bodily form. . . .[68]

Radbertus, on the other hand, sees miracles in much the same way he sees letters of the alphabet collectively constituting a meaningful text, viz., as durable existents adamantly independent of the mind of the observer. He understands the Eucharistic miracles he relates not as contraventions of an independent natural law but as direct, deliberate acts of God in a world already completely governed by precisely such acts.[69] He entertains no metaphysical mechanics of change but distinguishes simply what objects are at one moment from what they are at the next.

---

68. Augustine, *Genesis* XII.12.25.

69. As Miri Rubin put it: "The miraculous was widely perceived as part of nature which provided a paradigm for the explanation of the world and its apparent aberrations" (*Corpus Christi*, 112).

Beyond the Body

Because miracles are acts of God, there is no need for them to meet the requirements that ordinarily govern action and event, including those that demand visible evidence of change. This is particularly true of the miracle of miracles, the Incarnation, the invisible identity of man and God. Given Radbertus's literalist tendencies as an exegete with a strong propensity to interpret Scripture by Scripture, it is but a small step for him to recognize "This is my body" as divine notification of a miraculous event having occurred, one that has no more need of visible effect than did the Incarnation.

The Eucharistic miracles in Radbertus's *On the Body and Blood of the Lord* represent but a fraction of those that make up the tradition of such objects and events from the sixth century on up into the Reformation.[70] What is most striking about them, regardless of their subject matter—from seeing actual human flesh and tasting human blood in place of the Eucharistic elements to seeing the Christ child butchered on the altar—is that each is a manifestation, regardless of the form taken, of a stable reality, the original appearance of which can readily be restored when so bid.[71] It is the object itself that creates the conditions for its being seen, not the observing subject. Another constant element across the spectrum of such appearances is that they occur in response to doubt, for example, the doubt of the pious priest who only wants to see that he may believe.[72] For Radbertus Eucharistic miracles prove not only the invisible reality of a most sacred object but also its power. The most telling instance of this, despite its off-putting anti-Semitism, is the tale of the disbelieving Jew stricken with lockjaw by a consecrated host he had taken with sacrilegious intentions.[73] Miraculously suspended in his mouth, it can only be removed by the hand of the man of God. In this story as recounted by Radbertus, the status of the Eucharist as an object with power in its own right, as relic of the historical Christ, is firmly institutionalized. It is here and in the other miracle stories passed on by Radbertus that the basic question is posed as to what any object really is, a question that Berengarius will stumble on to his misfortune, and that scholastic philosophy over several centuries will labor by means of Aristotelian metaphysics to resolve.[74]

---

70. The most complete, categorically organized, catalog of these ever undertaken is that of Peter Browe. Of primary interest here are the miracles where the elements are transformed (verwandelt) into the bodily Christ (*Eucharistischen Wunder*, 93–100).

71. Radbertus, *De corpore et sanguine*, xiv, 89–90.

72. Ibid., xiv, 86–87.

73. Ibid., vi, 36–37.

74. As Marilyn McCord Adams notes, many of the philosophical issues that

"This Is" and the Transience of Intelligibility

Paradigms and Doctrines

That a shift in paradigms of knowledge in regard to Eucharistic belief took place over the ninth and tenth centuries is, again, at least in part indicated by the changes in reputation of the participants in the discussion. Despite warnings about excessively physical beliefs from not only Ratramnus but major figures like Hrabanus Maurus,[75] Radbertus's views would in time win the day. At a council held in Rome and at a synod held in Vercelli in 1050 to deal with the heresy of Beregarius, Ratramnus's treatise, misidentified as a by then lost work of Scotus Eriugena, was condemned and ordered burned,[76] as clear a judgment on the incompatibility of the figurative and physical doctrines of the Eucharist as one could wish. As often as such events have been considered steps in the development of the later doctrine of transubstantiation, however, it is plain that the shift involved is to a heavily physical rather than a *meta*physical understanding of the sacrament. We need look no further for "data" precipitating such a change than the number of obviously physical Eucharistic miracles, beginning with those cited by Radbertus as proofs against doubt and increasing almost exponentially over the succeeding centuries until materiality, as Carolyn Bynum describes, came to dominate late medieval religious practice.[77] And although the concept of substance in its more formal construals would eventually come to play a part in the theological explanations of sacramental change first insisted upon by Ratramnus, parties to those explanations quietly understood that their use of that term was not actually a referring one.[78] Further supporting

---

confronted the development of modern physical science had their debut in discussions of the Eucharist as a physical object: "And strange as it may seem to modern secular thinkers, medieval ideas about body were shaped as much by the constraints of this doctrine as by anything that Aristotle ever said. Indeed, philosophers continued to measure the adequacy of a philosophy of body in terms of its ability to make room for transubstantiation down to the seventeenth century when Descartes' theory is charged with a failure to do so" (*William Ockham*, 1:186–87).

75. Ratramnus of Corbie, *Ratramnus de corpore et sanguine*, 5–6.

76. Pelikan, *Christian Tradition*, 2:185–87, describes the succession of works that would over the next century establish the orthodoxy of Radbertus's position. Cf. also Macy, *Theologies of the Eucharist*, 35–36.

77. Bynum, *Christian Materiality*.

78. In Radbertus's own time Scotus Eriugena would declare *ousia* "incomprehensible" (Eriugena, *Periphyseon*, 3–4). Centuries later as philosophically opposite a figure as William of Ockham, would agree: ". . . no exterior corporeal substance can be cognized by us naturally in itself, whatever is [true] of the intellectual soul or any substance that pertains to the essence of the knower" (Adams, *William Ockham*, 1:541).

the plausibility of paradigm shift is the theoretical novelty, at least in the Latin West, of Radbertus's literalist hermeneutic, which would prove to be a durable alternative to the Augustinian theory of signs subscribed to by Ratramnus.

Characterizing extended and extensive changes in theological thinking as paradigm shifts or, to hew more closely to Kuhn's terminology, theological *revolutions*, has real merit as a heuristic device. With regard to the Eucharist it suggests that the mutual exclusivity of certain doctrinal views may originate not in their final, public forms but in intellectual presuppositions that refer experientially to very different ways of knowing the world, ways not unlike the "lifeworlds" of contemporary social theory. It also suggests, with regard to the Eucharist, that the high medieval doctrine of transubstantiation may be less directly concerned with explaining the sacrament than with coping with the religious consequences of a physical materialism that would in the end render the metaphysical notion of substance itself incomprehensible. Marilyn McCord Adams pointedly asks of that late scholastic debate whether transubstantiation was simply a "provoked ingenuity."[79] It further recommends that we recognize in the period from the ninth century to the Council of Trent in 1551 not the developmental "emergence" of a true doctrine but the unremitting repetition of what, from the adamantine declaration with which *On the Body and Blood of the Lord* begins, we might well call the Paschasian Canon: "*Christi communionem uerum corpus eius et sanguinem esse non dubitandum.*"[80] We cannot doubt that in sacramental communion we take the true body and blood of Christ.

Returning to the point from which we began, sea changes in the paradigms of knowledge that act as preconditions for religious experience can produce prima facie incompatible beliefs and doctrines. Doctrinal orthodoxy insists that of two such beliefs either one must be wrong or, leaning perhaps grudgingly on late modern notions of progress and development, an imperfect prefiguration of the other. We could easily encapsule these positions in the expressions "Different is wrong" and "Later is better." In periods of transition, of course, for which no definitive extent of time can be anticipated, we would expect to find compromise, contention, and ambiguity to be commonplace.

---

79. Adams, *Some Later Medieval* Theories, 87.

80 Pascasius Radbertus, *De corpore et sanguine domini*, 13.

"This Is" and the Transience of Intelligibility

But what can we really say about the beliefs of those living out of a paradigm of knowledge not our own? They may not prefigure later beliefs or resemble them in an identifiably nascent form. They may in fact not agree with them at all, were we to put the matter to the test. Further, if they do not agree, can we simply say they are wrong and dismiss them with an anathema? In his own day, Ratramnus appears to have enjoyed the height of respectability and, in fact, represented far more ably than Radbertus the patristic tradition that in the West had peaked in Augustine. At issue is whether there is a universal standard of orthodoxy that can bridge both history and differences as profound as those engendered by shifts in paradigms of knowledge. In practical terms, we can neither ignore nor condemn beliefs that differ on such foundational grounds, hold accountable those who, had they lived in later times, might have thought very differently.[81] But should there be no such standard of orthodoxy, what then constitutes either true belief or an identifiable tradition? Can there be other paradigms of knowledge, with correspondingly differently enabled beliefs about the Eucharist that could nonetheless claim our acceptance? Most directly, does the performative character of "do this" in the Eucharistic anamnesis suggest precisely another such paradigm of knowledge, one that ties us to neither an Augustinian idealism nor a physical realism? If so, we would need to accept it not as making a universal or eternal claim upon faith, but as representing, as was true of its predecessors described here, a new moment in a process of doctrinal development that resembles much more an evolutionary speciation than the progressive growth envisaged by nineteenth- and twentieth-century historians of doctrine.

---

81. Thus Jaroslav Pelikan: " . . . the effort to cross-examine the fathers of the second or third centuries about where they stood in the controversies of the ninth or sixteenth centuries is both silly and futile" (*Christian Tradition*, 1:267).

3

"DO THIS"—TEXT AND REPETITION

> For I did not imagine that things out of books would help me as much as the utterance of a living and abiding voice.
>
> —Papias of Hierapolis[1]

The Words of Jesus used in the Christian Eucharistic liturgy are institutionally words of Scripture. On one side, this certifies the indubitably Christian temper and history of the Words in the face of the great diversity of ritual practice in the ancient Christian world. It thus provides the form of the Words a canonical status that, once achieved, brooks no revisionary attempts to ameliorate their stark character through text-critical means of any sort. But being Scripture also exposes them to the difficulties attendant on that status, both those raised by the scholarly biblical-critical methods of the last several centuries and by more recent questioning about the relationship between historical events, written texts, and the truth-functional reliability of our experience with biblical, or for that matter, any writing.

---

1. Quoted in Eusebius, *History of the Church*, 102.

"Do This"—Text and Repetition

The Scandal of Hermeneutic Partisanship

Using "modern" in its historically extended sense, both the structure and the implicit intentions of modern biblical scholarship have proved somewhat ill-suited to the wants and needs of those professedly in search of a biblically-based faith. Text criticism of the eighteenth century made great strides in setting standards for textual reliability in the face of ongoing discoveries that had begun as early as the Reformation of textual variants, but at the expense of introducing uncertainty as to whether the biblical text as a whole could ever be as dependable a source of intellectual content as would be appropriate for documents claimed to be divinely inspired.[2] The hermeneutical higher criticism of the nineteenth century in all its many guises translated this quest for a perfect biblical text into rather one for the ultimate meaning of that text, whether found in its language, its sources, the literary intentions of those sources, or the intentions, literary or otherwise, of its authors. That quest continued on into the twentieth century, shaped additionally through the historical, philosophical, and, to date most successful, social researches that were that century's emblematic preoccupation.

For those considering themselves biblically-believing Christians, such modern critical researches necessarily challenged—and continue to challenge—the intrinsic authority of the revealed text. Less obviously, however, and perhaps more seriously, critical thinking about the Bible rests of its very nature on two implicit assumptions. The first is that criticism is necessary because we do not understand or know the meaning of the text. If its meaning were both clear and complete, after all, the critical enterprise would hardly be necessary. But ready access to a clear and complete meaning is essential to the ecclesial status of Scripture as a source of truths necessary for personal salvation. An esotericism that would make Scripture clear only to those predestined for such salvation offends not only against the notion that grace should be free for all, but that the ultimate purpose of revelation as a divine activity would have been designed from the start for at least a certain measure of frustration. The second is that, given even a low degree of textual uncertainty, criticism still must acknowledge the distance from the origins of Scripture that time, circumstance, oddities of linguistic usage, and human error in transmission have created, thus gifting it not only with an at best flawed authority but with an unresolvably incomplete

---

2. Most comprehensively described in Frei, *Eclipse*, 17–50.

knowability. The relationship of biblical criticism to a strong, uncritical, biblical faith is thus that of an intervention in a stipulated ignorance —ignorance of the text in its most authoritative possible form and an incorrigible, programmatic ignorance of its meaning. The biblical believer's often madrassa-like learning of the text in its public form, acquired through immense effort and with consuming devotion, can never achieve more than a fractured certainty. "Revelation" is destined thus to be the province of a few, a privileged scholarly elite. The continuum of skill and purpose that should exist between those who try to study Scripture and those who had achieved some degree of mastery in that effort is broken.[3] The angry alienation of biblicist believers from critical scholarship should come as no surprise.

The traditional path to certainty for the bible-believing Christian, however, is strewn with perils of its own. The structure of this certainty, determined early by Calvin, relies upon two specific instances of essentially supernatural activity on the part of the deity. One is the direct verbal inspiration of Scripture, meaning thereby that the Holy Spirit not only brought about the words of the text but is somehow coterminous or contiguous with them as a constantly available, living presence.[4] The second is that the same Holy Spirit acts in and upon believers in the tantalizingly quantifiable, event of "grace."[5] The necessary self-identity of the Spirit provides the only assurance necessary to support the belief that individual interpretation can reveal the meaning of a text with a reliability that mere scholarship can never hope to claim.

The principal difficulty faced, although seemingly not often enough, by the most biblically-oriented Christians is that calling on the Holy Spirit as a guarantor of particular meanings admits, even if not as candidly as critical scholarship does, that we could not otherwise have any reliable sense of what the text means. More perilously still, it involves calling up an invisible entity completely extraneous to the physical text in order to supply it with meaning on individually-tailored occasions, a maneuver not at all immune from the ancient, though still meaningful, strictures of Ockham's Razor. And finally, there will always be, as Calvin himself pointedly recognized, the possibility that what is thought to be the Spirit may be nothing more

---

3. As Kant, who was familiar with this problem, put it, " . . . historical faith must finally become mere faith in Scriptural scholars and their insight" (Kant, *Religion*, 105).

4. Calvin, *Institutes* I.7.4.

5. Ibid., II.3.12.

"Do This"—Text and Repetition

than the image of our own wishes and desires, not necessarily as worthy as they might be.[6]

Partisan attacks and counterattacks across the ideological divide between those considered to be liberals, academic elitists, or secularized intellectuals and those correspondingly categorized as conservatives, bible believers, or "ordinary" believers pay seemingly little attention to a set of problems about the text that both parties share, a problem for all texts and not just biblical ones. In the language of the mid-twentieth-century critical debate fostered by the self-styled "New Criticism," both groups seem all too often to fall prey to one or another of two errors, the "intentional fallacy" or the "affective fallacy."[7] The first identifies the intention of the author as the authoritative meaning of the text, while the second understands meaning to be realized in the effect that the text has on the reader.

Even though the first of these alleged fallacies of interpretation in particular has been seriously and thoughtfully challenged,[8] and the relativistic psychologism suggested by the second would not likely be taken seriously by many as a characterization of their belief, there remains the troubling issue of what is actually accomplished by any success they might have. Put most simply and directly, generically liberal and generically conservative approaches to the biblical text both assume that any interpretation produced represents an at least partial translational equivalent of the text itself. For the liberal, "partial" speaks to that dimension of classic texts that makes it possible for them to be powerfully meaningful in many different ways across time and history. For the conservative it means that there is no limiting the capacity of the Spirit as a provider of new meanings.

A hidden but substantial difficulty arises, however, when we consider that in either case the text itself vanishes in favor of and is replaced by its explanatory translations. In a lexical situation, of course, it should be respectable, if cumbersome, to substitute the definition of a term for the term itself in an assertion. We may, naturally, fuss some over whether the given definition is correct as it stands or needs semantic adjustment, but there are otherwise few, if any, reasons to question the logical propriety of such a substitution. But while this may satisfy lexical needs, it certainly does not work in situations where existence, expressed as quantification, is involved. At the most elementary level this means only that we should no more

---

6. Ibid., I.4.1,3,4.
7. Wimsatt and Beardsley, *Verbal Icon*, 3–18, 21–39.
8. Hirsch, *Validity*, 1–23.

expect to replace scriptural texts with hermeneutic ones than we should expect to make a meal of the definition of a chicken[9]. More seriously, it is clear that translational interpretations, no matter how meticulous in scholarly terms or respectful in intent, represent only a portion of the many possible options for what the text might be thought to mean, with no ultimate guarantee of either genuine adequacy or durable reliability. The Enlightenment aura of scientific authority that has unfortunately tended to cloak modern biblical scholarship has to some degree anaesthetized it against the fear and trembling that ought to trouble anyone who purports to "say the same as" a classic text, biblical or otherwise. That this is no new problem is amply demonstrated by the "semiotic anxiety" that afflicted both Origen and Augustine in the creation of their great commentary works.[10] The loss of the text by its vanishing into its interpretations, represents a step into a world where only the terms of the translational discussion may have value in themselves, where understanding the text is implicitly an affirmation of those values rather than the text itself.[11]

The Problem of the Poison Text

Such a discussion of the wrong-headedness of generic liberal and conservative approaches leads quite naturally to the question whether there is any effective way to approach a scriptural text, particularly that of the Eucharistic words, in a manner that is direct rather than epitomized, tautologized, dissipated, or, to reprise a Kierkegaardian complaint, "mediated" by interpretive techniques or idiosyncratic personal reflections.[12] Put in rather different terms, this question inquires about the possibility of an essentially

---

9. In logical terms, this simply notes that there are predicable differences between the tautology $x = x$ and the equivalence $x = y + z$ that become apparent under quantification in a situation where x is an object rather than a class thereof.

10. That Scripture was understood as divinely inspired or revealed rendered any interpretation of it utterly incommensurable with its meaning and thereby at constant risk, both intellectually and religiously. The polysemy of the biblical text represented not simply its cultural origins but the nature of revelation itself, as amply explained in Irvine, *Textual Culture*, 265–71.

11. A situation not unlike that once parodied by Ernest Gellner: "The (untrue) story is told that the Muslim conqueror of Alexandria ordered the burning of the books in the Library with the following argument: either the books say something other than the Koran—in which case they are false, or they say the same as the Koran—in which case they are redundant. In either case—burn them!" (Gellner, *Words and Things*, 198).

12. Kierkegaard, *Fear and Trembling*, 72–75, in regard to Luke 14:26.

"positivist" approach to the text that would have it stand, on its own, as an object of interest with even, perhaps, something we could call a "truth" or reliability of its own. This could in no way be simply noetic, signaling or representing a referential or interpretive equivalence, but would have to be "existential," essentially "bracketing" the undeniable existence of the text and even perhaps considerations of either its origins or demonstrated historical effects. But is it in the nature of a text, generically considered, to be so dealt with? And further, were we in fact able to isolate and identify a text in this way, what guarantee is there that doing so would produce not only any nontautologous results but even any results at all?

For the concept of text itself to be at issue is an ancient problem with an increasingly modern audience. What has been at stake consistently since the origins of the terms of the discussion in Plato has been the question whether writing is of any value whatsoever:

> The painter's products stand before us as though they were alive, but if you question them, they maintain a most majestic silence. It is the same with written words; they seem to talk to you as though they were intelligent, but if you ask them anything about what they say, from a desire to be instructed, they go on telling you just the same thing forever. And once a thing is put in writing, the composition, whatever it may be, drifts all over the place, getting into the hands not only of those who understand it, but equally of those who have no business with it; . . . And when it is ill-treated and unfairly abused it always needs its parent to come to its help, being unable to defend or help itself.[13]

On the face of it, this passage in the *Phaedrus* represents an uncharacteristically nominalist attack on the meaning of language, an attack enabled by an assumed difference between the same words whether as spoken or as written. Interpretation is demoted to mere repeating, and where nonredundant interpretation *is* attempted, catastrophe results should the interpreter be anyone but the author himself. No other distinction is made between the written and the spoken word than the active presence of the author as speaker, and the practical problem is left unaddressed whether spoken speech is not just as easily, if not perhaps even more easily, misunderstood than written. The coda of the *Phaedrus*, a prayer to Pan, appears to petition the divinity to the effect that physical things like written words never be allowed to corrupt or encumber the inner spirit's quest for wisdom.(279c)

13. Plato, *Phaedrus* 275d–e in *Collected Dialogues of Plato*.

Beyond the Body

The origin of these deprecations of writing appears at the outset of the dialog, where a deceitful Phaedrus attempts to repeat—allegedly from memory— an impressive speech on love by Lysias while cribbing it from a written copy hidden beneath his cloak.(228d) His hand forced by discovery of the deceit, Phaedrus then openly reads the speech. As a riposte Socrates gives a speech of his own, delivered supposedly spontaneously but with his head covered so that Phaedrus cannot see him speaking. (237a) Socrates begins with a familiar appeal to the Muses for assistance and breaks for breath somewhat later to exclaim how inspired he feels, how almost possessed he expects his speaking to become as he proceeds.(238c–d) Whether Socrates himself might have a text hidden beneath his own cloak is obviated by his later claim that he has covered his head for shame because of speaking so unworthily, so irreverently, of Love.(243b) This conceit is also accompanied by a quick jab at poets who write from experiences they have not in fact had: Stesichorus healed of his blindness once he admitted he had in fact not been at Troy to see the Helen he had so disparaged in writing. (243a–b)

It would be tempting to take most of the views about writing in the *Phaedrus* as particularly delicious Socratic ironies—a great writer lamenting in advance his future fate at the hands of critics—were it not for the much more serious and far-reaching condemnation of writing in 274c-275b, Socrates' tale of writing's mythical inventor, the Egyptian god Theuth. When Theuth presents writing to the king of Egypt as a new art for the people to grow in wisdom and memory, the king responds that exactly the opposite will occur: because they have writing, the people will never have to remember anything at all! Further, writing will enable them to think they know many things, none of which they will in fact have learned, leaving them with nothing but "the conceit of wisdom."(275b) Socrates' final rejoinder to Phaedrus about the myth is perhaps the most wholesale condemnation of literary culture ever penned:

> Then anyone who leaves behind him a written manual, and likewise anyone who takes it over from him, on the supposition that such writing will provide something reliable and permanent, must be exceedingly simple-minded; he must really be ignorant of Ammon's utterance if he imagines that written words can do anything more than remind one who knows of that which the writing is concerned with.[14]

---

14. Ibid., 275c.

"Do This"—Text and Repetition

Beyond the counterintuitive spectacle of a writer railing against writing, distrust of the written letter is a strong and very well established theme in Western critical thinking, from the Pauline admonition "for the letter kills, but the Spirit gives life" (2 Cor 3:6), to the dark remark of Jacques Derrida that "it goes without saying that the god of writing must also be the god of death."[15] The sense that the written text differs sufficiently from its spoken original to amount to having betrayed it plays a constant and unremitting counterpoint to the part of Western culture that, from the eleventh century onward, came to put both its public and its private trust increasingly in written documents.[16]

Attempts to deal with the seeming untrustworthiness of texts have been legion, from Stoic allegory and Christian mystical or anagogical interpretation to modern efforts, including this one, to rediscover a register of spoken speech that lies dormant, hidden, or obscured within writing itself.[17] Critics of literal-minded Protestantism suggest that fundamentalist readings of the biblical text solve the problems of uncertain or competing meaning by reducing the text to a mere icon, a quasi-sacramental sign that provides occasion for the Holy Spirit to fill the mind of the reader with appropriate thoughts. Thus David Morgan:

> . . . the use of the red-letter, or rubricated, Christian Bible, which marks the spoken words of Jesus in red type, is a noteworthy instance of the way some modern Protestants experience the iconicity of the biblical text. They read the red portions of the Gospels with a special sense of being close to Jesus, reinfusing the written word with the status of utterance, the phonic presence of the speaker. Signaled visually, the red-letter text urges devout readers to hear the sound of their voice reading Christ's words as the sound of his voice.[18]

Students of Plato, particularly those who rediscovered his works in the Renaissance, proposed to solve the problem by opining that he had been venting his pique not at the enterprise of writing in general but at alphabetic writing which, in contrast to the hieroglyphic writing of ancient

---

15. Derrida, "Plato's Pharmacy," 91.

16. Cf. Stock, *Implications of Literacy*, 14–17.

17. Thus Catherine Pickstock, who turns to doxological and liturgical use as practical examples of how the text can be encountered as itself rather than as the *nachlass* of interpretation (*After Writing*, 220–52).

18. Morgan, *Sacred Gaze*, 10.

Egypt, represents the sounds of words rather than the objects to which the words refer:

> The Greeks use language, like pedants, merely as empty words to argue with; the Egyptian, or magical, use of language or signs is for communicating directly with divine reality, "capturing the language of the gods, . . ."[19]

Tantalizingly, in the dialog *Theaetetus* (142a–143b) Plato himself seems to provide a solution to the problem of the *Phaedrus* by demonstrating the proper way to draft a text that re-presents, as it were, an earlier discussion.[20] Two friends, Euclides and Terpsion, newly returned from traveling, meet each other just as Theaetetus, from whom the dialog gets its name, is being carried home from the wars, dying. The friends lament his condition and heap praise upon his character, recalling in particular the high opinion Socrates had of him when he was young. Terpsion asks about the original conversation Socrates had had with Theaetetus and whether Euclides can repeat it. Euclides replies that were he forced to rely upon memory alone he could not but, fortunately, he took notes on the discussion, carefully adding to these as he remembered more over time. Eventually he wrote out the entire text, taking care as well to check its accuracy with Socrates on several occasions. With no further ado, and sadly no further interest in the mortal fate of Theaetetus himself, the friends then proceed to have a slave read the written text of the dialog to them in their leisure.[21]

Traditionally, the *Theaetetus* has been viewed primarily as a study of problems in the nature of knowledge. The initial inclusion of Theodorus, a geometer, in the discussion suggests there may indeed be some truths that are durably reliable and dependably certain. The argument, however, in which Theodorus as it happens takes little part, proceeds with Socrates'

---

19. Yates, *Giordano Bruno*, 264.

20. Reading the *Theaetetus* as a sequel to the *Phaedrus* and in fact as part of a trilogy that concludes in the *Republic* follows the view of Schleiermacher on the sequence of these works as originally composed. See Lamm, "The Art of Interpreting Plato," 106–7.

21. It is, parenthetically, difficult to think the author of the first chapter of the Gospel of Luke ignorant of the compositional process Euclides describes. His implicit criticism of what must have been the text of Mark (Lk 1:4) and his insistence on the necessity for a broader, narrative, setting of the sayings and *res gestae* of Jesus suggest that he saw the text of his gospel as innovative theological literature rather than an as report or chronicle. That critical reflection on the nature of historical writing was a long-standing preoccupation of the ancient world is evident as well in the writings of Lucian of Samosata (c. 120 –c. 190 CE), particularly the *How to Write History*.

"Do This"—Text and Repetition

typical elenchic doggedness to prove that no such certainties are possible. Well toward the end of the dialog Socrates turns to the "science" of arithmetic, understanding by this knowing something about numbers and about the odd and even.(198a) Complaining that possessing the knowledge of individual numbers is as fleeting as possessing captive birds, in *Theaetetus* 198d Socrates takes up again the position held in *Phaedrus* 275c, that in either counting or *reading*, rather than actually learning anything, we simply set about learning again from ourselves what we already knew. To this Theaetetus replies that he had heard from another thinker that

> ... true belief with the addition of an account (*logos*) was knowledge, while belief without an account was outside its range. Where no account could be given of a thing, it was not 'knowable'—that was the word he used—where it could, it was knowable.[22]

At this point Plato begins to indulge wholeheartedly his general fascination with writing, particularly with its most basic elements, letters and syllables,[23] recasting the discussion as an inquiry into whether we can, through those, acquire knowledge. He concludes through detailed argument for each that neither a combination of syllables, nor a combination of letters, nor of single syllables, nor of single letters are the stuff of which an account (*logos*) can plausibly be made. Socrates then proposes three criteria for an account, neatly summarized as: 1) the image of thought in spoken sound, 2) an enumeration of all the elements that make up a whole, and 3) a list of everything that is different or distinguishing about something.(208c) Sadly, each of these fails, at least in part on the grounds of circularity, i.e., that we must already have a clear understanding of knowledge in mind in order to apply them.

The *Theaetetus* concludes with the predictable declaration by Socrates that while a reliable account of knowledge continues to elude the participants, and to elude Socrates himself in particular, the discussion has yet been worthwhile. We have come to know, as a result of Socratic midwifery,

---

22. *Theaeteus* 201d.

23. In *Philebus* 18b–c he sketches the particulars of Theuth's invention of alphabetical writing, while in the *Sophist* he enlists the help of Theaetetus again, this time in dialog with the Eleatic Stranger, to deal with problems about spelling and grammar. *Statesman* 277e–278d describes the process of learning to read. In *Cratylus* he turns, with almost illogical abandon, to the adumbration of etymologies. For further on this point: Ryle, "Letters and Syllables in Plato," 431–51 and Gallop, "Plato and the Alphabet," 364–76. Regarding the relation between "sound" and "sense," see Holland, "An Argument in Plato's *Theaetetus*," 97–116.

just what and how much we do not know, acquiring thereby an admirable humility with which to address future philosophical questions. Some religious sentiments surface in the allusion to midwifery as a gift from heaven (210c), but the devout prayer to Pan at the end of the *Phaedrus* is missing here. Socrates rather leaves hurriedly to keep his appointment at court to defend himself against the charges for which he will later be condemned. More pointedly, we are left stranded regarding whatever effect the dialog may have had on Terpsion and Euclides, i.e., the original dramatic setting has simply been abandoned. The results of the dialog are three in number: that Theaetetus became a better man because of it, that owing to the silence of the text about them, Terpsion and Euclides did not, and that the superiority of spoken speech and dialectic over an epistemologically foundationless written text has been established.

It would be easy to dismiss Plato's reservations about writing as a medium for conveying thought on the grounds that they represent nothing more than his obsession with the abstract and ideal as the epitome of truth, inevitably in combat against the practical necessities of human communication. It is more difficult to deny, however, that his destruction of any theoretical basis for a sure and certain correspondence of text and thought, whether author's *or* reader's, lies at the heart of the fundamental disagreements that divide the contemporary community of those who interpret Scripture professionally. Plato's essentially nominalist view of writing makes it impossible for the text to be more than a signal that speech has somehow occurred and a starting flag for treating that event as something for discussion. The distance of text from an original speech event, whether oral or mental, explains to some degree the capacity of classic texts to be read very differently from generation to generation of scholarship. But it also raises the specter of a Diltheyian relativism about the historical circumstances of both the text and the interpreter. Recalling the question posed at the outset, is there any effective way to approach a text, in particular the Scriptural text of the Eucharistic words, in a manner that is direct rather than sucked dry of its worth by interpretation, whether scholarly or devout? If we take Plato seriously about this, the answer is clearly that there is not. But if we consider more deeply the temporal aspects of the relationship of word to text, perhaps there is.

"Do This"—Text and Repetition

The Letter that Gives Life

Owing to the circumstances of its utterance, there is prima facie no reason to think that the request of Jesus at the Last Supper to be remembered, strikingly different though it was from so much else in the synoptics,[24] was addressed to any but those few who were present rather than to the many who would later follow them.[25] On what grounds, we might well ask, did that very local and particular request later come to be universalized in both practice and doctrine?

It has been perceptively remarked that claims to the preeminence of scripture need to be tempered by the realization that there was a time *before* scripture, a time when local Christian traditions bore the burden of maintaining and transmitting the message about Jesus.[26] The earliest evidence for the existence of this is 1 Cor 11:1, where Paul commends his audience because they "remember me in everything and maintain the traditions just as I handed them on to you."[27] In the face, however, of instances among the Corinthians where those traditions, and in particular the tradition of Eucharistic practice, had begun to go astray, Paul restates what he "received from the Lord" and "handed on to you" in a carefully worded, formulaic recital of the words of the Last Supper (1 Cor 11:23–26) that would later be reprised in the more narrative setting of Luke 22:17–19.

Tradition, in the sense that 1 Corinthians uses it, had plainly taken shape in oral form on divers occasions over an extended period of time. But that oral form, consisting in its entirety of precisely those original utterances that, on a Platonic understanding of the relation between utterance and writing ought to have been most authoritative, thereby lacked the power to shape a coherent and consistent religious practice. Although it is quite easy to hear the fallible voice of a living Paul in the text of his more culturally-oriented admonitions in 1 Corinthians 11, it is equally difficult

---

24. So different, in fact, that their authenticity has sometimes been doubted. See Schweitzer, *Problem*, 57–62 and idem, *Quest*, 66. Schweitzer attributed this view as well to Schleiermacher, whose wholehearted endorsement of the fourth gospel over the synoptics as historical witness to Jesus led him to considerable skepticism over the authenticity of the Eucharistic anamnesis or "Wiederholungsbefehl."

25. See Heaney, "Memorial," 450–59.

26. ". . . for there was a tradition of the church before there was ever a New Testament, or any individual book of the New Testament" (Pelikan, *Jesus*, 10).

27. Paul similarly refers to "tradition" (*paradosis*) in Gal 1:14, Col 2:8, and 2 Thess 2:15 and 3:6.

to dismiss the normative formality of his description of the Eucharistic anaphora, particularly because it is given not as speech but in writing, in a letter, as text. From the standpoint of orthodoxy, that the tradition has now become text gives it fixity. Such a point of view is sustainable, however, only if we accept that text can somehow embody an ideal "meaning" in a manner that makes that meaning one, unchangeable, and readily accessible. But this is precisely the difficulty with text that Plato was most adamant about, viz., that such a meaning resides exclusively in the orality of original speech and can only be betrayed by text.

What, then, can the textual formulation of a tradition accomplish that the living word cannot? The most obvious rejoinder to this is that orality is limited intrinsically to the time and place of original utterance, while text can outlive its author and, ages hence, visit places the text never, so to speak, dreamed of. Again, while orality addresses a frangible living audience, text can address many audiences in contexts like silent reading, reading aloud, and by being heard in, among other circumstances, liturgical settings. When we consider that language, and by extension, original utterance, are part of natural human behavior, albeit refined and polished by human convention, writing is in contrast entirely conventional, a social phenomenon driven by the human need to communicate as durably as possible over time and distance. It is because, therefore, of text that the request of Jesus at the Last Supper to be remembered by doing "this" can engage an audience beyond those in the Last Supper room.

How can it be, however, that those words, conveyed by text, can actually constitute an appeal over time, place, and the centuries from one individual to other, later individuals who may hear or read them? The first point in this regard is that any particular collection of words uttered at a specific moment in time implies the possibility as a class of an indefinite, and therefore potentially infinite, number of lexically identical utterances. What was said can be repeated, although with the very real caveat that the original moment itself as an instance in time cannot. For every utterance, particularly for those with the formulaic cast of 1 Cor 11:23–26, an infinite number of possibilities can arise for it to be repeated, assuming for the sake of argument the adequacy of translation.[28] A second point relates to the fact that requests, appeals, and even orders do not necessarily cease

---

28. Or, in the words of Jean-Luc Marion, "... an infinity of Eucharists, celebrated by an infinity of different communities, each of which leads a fragment of the words back to the Word" (*God Without Being*, 157).

to be effective just because the one making them has left the scene, either momentarily or historically, and they can often be more durable in their effect than the intentions of the one who made them. The debts we owe to others live on after they are gone. Tasks left by parents to children remain as obligations after the former have departed life, and they may extend even to those children's children. Those of a metaphysical bent might consider this an instance of Kant's categorical imperative at work. Those less so inclined might call to mind Wittgenstein's remark to the effect that to live in the present is in fact to be eternal.[29] A third point takes into consideration the uses of text in legal contexts, specifically in agreements, where a written contract serves in fact to *convey* the agreement of the parties to any and all in any later circumstances where that agreement may apply. The text of 1 Cor 11:23–26 conveys the request to "do this" to all of those in both its real and its possible audiences, conveying as well an obligation for them to respond.

But if the continuing life of the tradition is in the letter of the text, how does the repetition of that text escape from the unproductive redundancy that, on Plato's terms, can never attain to more than an iconic meaning?

Repetition

The request to "do this" has as its most obvious fulfillment a repeat performance of the collective actions and forms of words given most completely in 1 Cor 11:23–26. Doing these is in effect to accomplish what those words describe, but it still leaves open many possible issues about how that might occur and, consequently, what it might achieve. For example, is it simply a copying or duplication of a set of words and actions? In that case, of what real use could it be given that, as Socrates complained, written words "seem intelligent, but if you ask them anything about what they say, . . . they go on telling you just the same thing forever"? (*Phaedrus* 275d) More positively, is it a historical reenactment of the narrative, a dramatic presentation for an audience, a recreation of a state of affairs, or an attempt to recapture the frame of mind of Jesus or the disciples in those hallowed moments? Might it even be an attempt to escape the restraints of time and history to a cosmic plane where all moments are but a single instant in the paradoxical timelessness of eternity, a preview of eternal life?

29. " . . . dann lebt er ewig, der in der Gegenwart lebt" (Wittgenstein, *Tractatus*, 146), perhaps better translated as " . . . he lives forever who lives in the present."

Beyond the Body

The concept of repetition has been the object of considerable serious attention, particularly in French philosophy.[30] It was originated by Kierkegaard, in that central portion of his work that began with the multiple retellings of Abraham's sacrifice of Isaac (Gen 22) in *Fear and Trembling* (1843).[31] That the same event could be cast so differently in successive descriptions laid the groundwork for those doubts about historicity that would culminate in the great questions of the *Philosophical Fragments* (1844) and the *Concluding Unscientific Postscript to the Philosophical Fragments* (1846): "Is a historical point of departure possible for an eternal consciousness," and whether "it is possible to base an eternal happiness upon historical knowledge."[32]

Published simultaneously with *Fear and Trembling*, Kierkegaard's *Repetition: An Essay in Experimental Psychology* took as its task to explore repetition both as a philosophical concept and as a characteristic pattern of human activity, whether physical, artistic, or social.[33] The philosophical question leads with a distinction between recollection for the ancient Greeks and repetition for the modern world as primary modes of thought. Recollection is, of course, Plato's doctrine, promoted most notably in the dialog *Meno*, of the soul's knowledge of the Ideas prior to birth. The excellence of recollection is that it provides the certainty, clarity, and beauty of ultimate truth. The pain of recollection is that in comparison to the objects of recollection ordinary realities strike us as banal to the point of utter disgust. Because of this, recollection makes us unhappy, leading a life in which we seem always to have "forgotten something." Oddly, though by no means paradoxically, "the love of recollection is the only happy love," but only if what we love is the ideal and not the stuff of later experience.[34] The philosophical concept of recollection has as its counterpart in daily life the

30. See especially Deleuze, *Difference*, 70–128.

31. Kierkegaard, *Fear and Trembling*, 9–14.

32. Kierkegaard, *Philosophical Fragments*, title page; restated in idem, *Concluding Unscientific Postscript*, 18.

33. "Repetition belongs to the world of natural phenomena, and it is a mistake to transfer it to the world of spirit" (Kierkegaard, "Open Letter to Professor Heiberg," in *Fear and Trembling*, 286).

34. Kierkegaard, *Repetition*, 33. *Repetition* was itself a literary experiment, a fictional narrative in the form of a detective story related by the pseudoauthor as investigator. Both the device and the extravagant style reflect the romantic influence of the E. T. A. Hoffman circle. Although it is unlikely that Kierkegaard would at this point (1843) have read E. A. Poe's "The Murders in the Rue Morgue" (1841), some indication of a passing interest in crime and punishment in America appears in the preface to the *Postscript*, 5.

"Do This"—Text and Repetition

idealization of historical events or past experiences, with the result that the present counterparts of those events or experiences can only be found lacking. The pain of the young man whose romance is central to the narrative of *Repetition* is that every attempt he made to recapture his original love for the object of his affections led him to despair. In the larger Kierkegaardian frame of reference, this meant that he had enjoyed the aesthetic aspects of love but had mistakenly tried to idealize them, to fatal effect. Out of this conflict arises the ethical question whether he can continue with or marry someone whom he loved in a historical past that is no longer available except through recollection, "a discarded garment that does not fit."[35]

As a mode or habit of thought, recollection poses formidable dangers for both the individual religious life and its ecclesial counterpart. Idealization of splendid liturgical celebrations experienced in the past can readily be seen to trivialize those of the present, perforce engendering a culture of disappointment and coping. The present can, of course, be bracketed and life lived in the idealized past, an analgesic reaction that dulls the pain of comparison but all too easily morphs into a sybaritic and dysfunctional romanticism. In Kierkegaard's words, " . . . he who would only recollect is a voluptuary."[36] But anecdotally reported individual experiences of joy and even exaltation as in, e.g., taking communion, are not infrequently followed by periods of *acedia* and despair, a well-known phenomenon of the spiritual life. The text of the Eucharistic anaphora is likewise capable of being idealized, semiotically fixed as a marker for an individually revealed meaning, subject nonetheless to the perils of historicity. And any attempt to idealize the texts of 1 Corinthians 11:23–26 or Luke 22: 17–20 in a mental image of the event described, could not escape the limits imposed by the scope and idiosyncrasy of the individual imagination. As Kierkegaard so tellingly suggested, not even those contemporary to such events can do without faith.[37] Finally, although the Western religious tradition's consistent adherence to an *ex opere operato* doctrine of sacramental action immures it in principle from the mental vagaries of officiating clergy, there is no doubt that the habits of thought associated with recollection could have telling effects on

---

35. Kierkegaard, *Repetition*, 34.

36. Ibid. John of the Cross makes the same point in describing the beginner in the spiritual life as prone to "luxury" and "gluttony" (John of the Cross, *Dark Night*, 47–52, 53–58).

37. " . . . a knowledge of all the circumstances, with the reliability of an eye-witness, does not make such an eye-witness a disciple. . . ." (Kierkegaard, *Philosophical Fragments*, 73).

Beyond the Body

congregational life, the emergence of a mercilessly uncompromising traditionalism among them.

But while recalling the concept of recollection wakes in us comfortable associations with a familiar ancient doctrine, this is certainly not the case with repetition. For one thing, repetition is an intentionally innovative notion, one that developed out of both Kierkegaard's oft-stated dislike of Hegelianism and his much less obvious struggle with the heritage of Kant. This is a development, however, that he would be naturally loathe to admit, implying as it does the origins of the notion of repetition from two diametrically opposed positions on mental life: the Hegelian view of mind as a fluid field of ongoing clash between thoughts and concepts that produces creative resolutions superior to their origins, and the Kantian transcendental self with its omniscient point of view and fixed *a priori* categories of perception and judgment.[38] His objection to the Hegelian dialectic as a philosophy of mind, which he understands as "mediation," is based both on the evidence of his own thought experiments in *Repetition* and his acceptance of the Aristotelian doctrine that something cannot come from nothing,[39] i.e., that change is not substantially productive or evolutionary but in some manner accretive. Mediation, like recollection, loses the past in a present that is forever alienated from it. His debt to Kant reveals itself in his later description of repetition as a "category," a term that clearly reflects Kant's understanding of category as a realm of experiencing rather than a collective term for kinds of things experienced.[40] His unstated objection to Kant seems to be that there is no room in the Kantian system for psychological growth and change, only accumulated reaction to external circumstances, both sensible and ethical. To some degree this is also a covert consideration of doubts about causality raised earlier by Hume in the *Treatise on Human Nature* (1739) and *An Inquiry Concerning Human Understanding* (1777), doubts that Kant summarized but rejected in the *Critique of Pure Reason* (1781) in favor of assigning causality to the category of necessity, thus intellectualizing it.[41] *Repetition* sees Kierkegaard searching for a way to describe a positive, progressive, psychological process in which past events, though

---

38. Kierkegaard's dilemma here is that treating repetition as the resolution of conflict between two concepts is *eo ipso* to accept the validity of "mediation."

39. Kierkegaard, *Philosophical Fragments*, Interlude 1, 90–93.

40 Kierkegaard, *Postscript*, 235: "The category of repetition is at bottom an expression for immanence. . . . " See also Kierkegaard, *Repetition*, 52. For Kant's description of the categories, see Kant, *Critique*, 113–14.

41. Kierkegaard, *Postscript*, 44–45.

in principle lost to us, remain a contributing part of the ongoing narrative of life.

The literary extravagance of *Repetition* makes it difficult to parse its philosophical content in "proper" critical fashion. Its pseudonymous author, one "Constantine Constantius," deflects at every turn any insight we might imagine we have into Kierkegaard's own purposes as the real author. Fortunately, "do this . . . " can be repeated in several distinctly different kinds of circumstances that materially affect our expectations of its intent and the logic of its consequences, and these do provide a way forward. We can characterize these uses generically, with some predictable possibility of overlap, as *redundant, ritual, historical,* and *dramatic.*

Redundant

The words of the text can, most basically, simply be said again as a whole, relying either upon a written text for their form or upon memory. The social dimensions of this situation include first of all the acceptance of text itself as a medium of communication, and that *this* text can, at the very least, be physically readable and intellectually intelligible. At such an essentially nominalist level it does not really matter what the text is a text *of.* Reading something over to oneself is the paradigmatic, though not the only example of such verbal repetition.[42]

Ritual

The text can be read—and heard—aloud in either a ceremonial or a liturgical context, accepted as the text *of* something with an institutionally agreed historical identity. Acceptance of a text in such a situation presumes its "authenticity," whether established through the social enterprise of scholarship, through personal conviction, or through decision by a church. Both historical and personal dimensions enjoy a particularly polysemous relation to the text. For critical scholarship the historicity of a text can be embedded internally in the form of the words itself or, externally, through

---

42. Deleuze refers to this as "bare, material repetition" (*Difference,* 21). Alain Badiou recognizes that repetition of this sort is not entirely without its usefulness, as in Deleuze's endless similar cases of cinematic analysis that, compounded, begin to demonstrate of themselves a theory of cinema. Badiou refers to these under the heading of "monotonous productions" (Badiou, *Deleuze,* 13).

description in greater or lesser detail of the circumstances in which it originated. Historicity establishes what the text is a text *of*. Personal acceptance of authenticity is of its nature more tenuous, relying as it does upon personal states at particular times. The form of the letters remains, but feeling for them may or may not, owing to either longer-term changes in personal history or to an emotional inability to be appreciative that is part of the regular come-and-go of the spiritual life. Text as formally read evokes historicity, including that of any church body that has sanctioned such a reading. Text as heard is bound to a moment that will itself become historical as it becomes part of the past. As read text enjoys the advantages of fixity, but always under the threat of potential inauthenticity. As heard text reprises in kind its original utterance, but not that original event. Ritual includes the presumption of *meaning*, but always at the threat of potential historicity.

Historical

The text "do this" can also be read, recited, or dramatically played in circumstances of historical re-enactment. The conditions for this include stringent requirements on the authenticity of the text and on the physical circumstances in which the re-enactment is made to take place. But, perhaps most of all, it demands cultivation of a frame of mind that places the participant, whether speaker, hearer, or silent actor, within the original events. The similarity as a mental project of re-enactment to recollection provides ample warning of the danger that historicity poses for it.

Dramatic

Text is also repeated, without the overtones of ceremony or liturgy, on the theatre stage and, by extension, in film. As an action it is directed to an audience for one of several purposes. Serious drama can aim to please aesthetically by the construction of the text, epitomized perhaps in those lines of drama that strike us most by reason of their elegance of phrase and nobility of description. It can also deliberately rouse reaction in its hearers for investigative purposes or to promote ethical concerns by depicting central characters who serve as ethical lessons for us all. As Aristotle noted in the *Poetics*, perhaps somewhat cynically, drama raises in its audience pity for the fate of another like ourselves and a concomitant fear that the same could happen to us. Historicity and authenticity affect dramatic text primarily in ways familiar to "text criticism," e.g., the manuscript tradition of the play, its performance tradition as it has affected the transmission of the text and, finally, attribution of authorship.

Across the narrative landscapes of *Repetition* Kierkegaard pursues a definition of that concept in a myriad of instances—dimly glimpsed in some, clearly intuited in others, beguilingly mysterious for the most part. The difficulty of the task is owing, perhaps, to two factors. The first, a primarily historical one, is that in the literary architectonic of Kierkegaard's work repetition plays the role of a trope, a literary device that corresponds to and represents a movement of thought. Where the forms of the syllogism fix the most basic elements of reasoning in Aristotle's Organon, so too for Kierkegaard repetition describes the most elemental form of thought discernible in all mental, or spiritual, change and progress. But though foundational as a concept, repetition remains ever only the passing form of thoughts, never their content, a constant and reliable "turn of thought" always at hand but seldom mentioned on the way to higher goals. The second factor is that Kierkegaard was invariably anxious to avoid being thought a "systematic" thinker, one whose basic assumptions could be cataloged, epitomized, and critically dismantled, as had been the fate of Descartes, Leibniz, and even Kant, in his own time. He thus defines repetition ostensively through instances of it rather than terminologically.[43] The only critical proviso allowed is the judgment as to whether, or to what degree, it has been effective.

Kierkegaard recognizes the sort of verbal repetition we have labeled "redundant" while succeeding in paying it only as much attention as it deserves. In a most basic instance he notes that saying "No!" repeatedly can add nothing whatever to the original utterance,[44] a sentiment certainly reminiscent of Plato. More expansively, he cites the example of a preacher who uses the identical sermon on two successive Sundays, something that seemingly no one, including the preacher himself, takes note of. Because it has no consequences, has brought about no difference, a repetition like this has no status as an event. In contrast, the teacher who repeats an admonition to a student and attaches a grade to it has indeed produced

---

43. "When a classification does not ideally exhaust its object, a haphazard classification is altogether preferable, because it sets the imagination in motion" (Kierkegaard, *Repetition*, 66).

44. Ibid., 97.

consequences. In this case we can properly talk of a repetition because it is an event that brings a succeeding situation into existence, such that "what has been now becomes,"⁴⁵ i.e., "a transition from not existing to existing."⁴⁶ Lastly, there is the case of the student who, baffled by the incompleteness of "the system," reads and rereads a philosophical text, translates it into his mother tongue, learns much of it by heart, outlines its arguments, makes set after set of notes, and in the end buys a new copy of the book so as not to be reminded of his prior bafflements. His efforts still remain fruitless, but only up to that point when he elects to rest content with both simply admiring the author and accepting his own limitations.⁴⁷

Although Kierkegaard evinced only a modicum of formal interest in ritual and liturgy during his life and, similarly, appeared less than impressed with the pomp of civil ceremony, his narrative in *Repetition* of a trip to Berlin undertaken in an attempt to repeat all the conditions of an earlier visit there reveals considerable sensitivity to the details of ritual action:

> One ascends a flight of stairs in a house illuminated by gas, one open a small door, one stands in the vestibule.... One goes straight ahead, one finds oneself in an antechamber.... A branch candlestick stands on the writing table, beside which stands a handsome armchair covered with red velvet.... One sits down on a chair by the window, one looks out upon the great square....⁴⁸

But despite all the enforced similarities of the second visit to the first, his stay in the same lodgings failed as a repetition, merely because the proprietor of the premises had in the meantime married. Neither the carefully crafted ritual of entry nor the attempted duplication of historical circumstances succeeded in producing a true repetition. Neither ritualistic nor historical replication could supply the certainty that a true repetition would require.

It is in describing his experience of the theatre that Kierkegaard waxes most eloquent and correspondingly lets slip somewhat the cloak with which he habitually conceals his philosophic interests. Berlin, he tells us, as though quoting from a travel guide, has three theatres. The Opera House presents both operas and ballets that, when successful, the audience finds pleasing, even "splendid." The Dramatic Theatre presents works "that are for

---

45. Ibid., 52.
46. Kierkegaard, *Philosophical Fragments*, 91.
47. Kierkegaard, *Postscript*, 17.
48. Kierkegaard, *Repetition*, 55–56.

instruction and culture, not merely for pleasure." But it is the third theatre, the Königstädter, famous for its production of farces, that he finds most to his liking, owing especially to a memorable performance of Nestroy's *Der Talisman* that he had seen on an earlier visit. Patrons of the Königstädter do not expect to be pleased or instructed, but to be entertained.[49] The parallel of the first two of these institutions to the aesthetic and the ethical described in *Fear and Trembling* raises quite naturally the expectation that a discussion of farce will bear religious significance.

Recalling that earlier performance with near boundless enthusiasm, Kierkegaard embarks upon a lengthy panegyric on theatre. Although he never mentions specifically the relation of the printed text of a drama to its performance(s), the first great image of the discussion, the constant wind of the mountains, focuses on the meaninglessness of repeating where nothing new, nothing additional is created. But the ceaseless noise of the wind never fails to awaken in the mature individual a sense of personal identity, a sense that one has one's own particular experiences in a life that wind—and text—impinge upon but can never totally possess.[50] The succession of images that follows explores in turn the mature spectator who attempts, in effect, to rob the play of its content for purposes of explanation, the writer who imagines he has a great deal to say until he tries to do so, and a kitsch painting that, while attractive, conveys little more than flatulent generalities. Of these three, only the latter holds anything of value, in that those generalities may recall individual experiences that, though personal, have been had by many.[51]

The proper audience for farce at the Königstädter is neither patrons of opera and ballet nor critics of serious theatre. Rather it is common people who are there to enjoy themselves, to be entertained, and who, seemingly without a care and immersed simply and without reservation in the moment, bear a remarkable resemblance to the character of the Knight of Faith in *Fear and Trembling*. They go with no prior expectation of either pleasure or instruction; they have no specific need to admire the show, or even to laugh at or be touched by it.[52] The plot that will unfold before them in *Der Talisman* is rife with humorous and highly unlikely situations that

---

49. Ibid., 57–58.

50. Ibid., 59, thus giving rise, perhaps, to what Deleuze calls the "narcissistic ego" (*Difference*, 110–11).

51. Kierkegaard, *Repetition*, 60–62.

52. Ibid., 63.

both reflect some of the ironies of life and yet also pose the question how they themselves would react to them. The characters are of two sorts, one a collection of stereotypical roles and the other, needing only one or two, the kind of comic geniuses whose task is to bring the farce alive. They do this not by that fidelity to the text that opera and serious drama require, but by living it in the moment. The great actress "rushes upon the stage with a country landscape behind her," not as painted backdrop but as if in the train of her dress. The great actor is the one who "can come walking," not repeating the steps of walking but becoming himself his entrance into the scene. These are not easy things to do, because they are haunted by the peril of failure into the trite, the banal, the ordinary.[53] Were they to fail, the moment in which actors and audience live together the absurdities of the play could not occur.

Alas, Kierkegaard's expectations of the Königstädter on his second visit to Berlin were to be tragically disappointed. His old seat was unavailable, the theatre was crowded, the audience was bored, and comic genius was sadly lacking in the performance. Undaunted, he nonetheless returned to the Königstädter again the following evening, only to find his continuing hopes for a repetition dashed by yet another disappointment. Totally frustrated, he returned to Copenhagen in the belief that his lodgings, at least, would have remained the same in his absence and thus provide an experience of repetition. Alas, his butler had undertaken a major housecleaning in his absence.[54]

The Moment

Literary distance allows us to see what Kierkegaard's pseudonymous author Constantine Constantius cannot, viz., that attempting a repetition cannot produce one. The second trip to Berlin was based foremost upon a *recollection* of the experiences of the first trip and, hence, was in principle bound to fail. Although circumstances changed, Constantius proved true to his name, unchangeable. One attempt fails after another, thwarting ever anew the hope that a historical recreation of places, events, and situations is possible. In only one instance does anything occur that offers any hope, namely, that when going to the same restaurant every evening he hears the

---

53. Ibid., 68.
54. Ibid., 74–76.

same greetings and farewells of its regular guests as they arrive and leave. A repetition, yes, but an undeniably trivial one.[55]

Despite its wealth of psychological detail, *Repetition* actually leaves a great deal unsaid about the first trip to Berlin, particularly about the marvelous first evening at the Königstädter. What are we to make, for instance, of the juxtapositioning of farce with the religious, when opera and comedy fill, respectively, the roles of the aesthetic and the ethical? Why was the recollection of this evening so important, given that nothing more exceptional occurred than entertainment, especially that of the poorer, less cultured, patrons? What defines the special character of the evening, and why does it have such a continuing influence on the life of the author? The primary thing to consider, easily overlooked, is that the performance of the play is first, though not foremost, a recital, a repeating of its text. A popular comedy of the period, there is nothing about *Der Talisman* that suggests beauty, ethical grandeur, or religious fervor.[56] The relationship of text to play is quite simply that the text is a necessary but not sufficient condition for the performance, little more than a *sine qua non* for an indefinite number of possible readings or performances. Plays with similar plot and characters could, of course, be performed spontaneously, i.e., without text, but only those based on the text—at least to some degree—can claim its name and/or its authorship.[57] The text exists not as the play itself but as an indispensable and enabling condition for performances. The text is that which, before all others, makes the occurrence of the event of the play possible.

As an event, a performance of the play, although it becomes such only really with the closing curtain, is not yet the historical point of departure for any and all recollections of it. At the time it is seemingly self-contained, at least in the manner that events are commonly characterized as having a cause or causes and a before and an after.[58] But so narrow a construal of event, while it provides an at least temporally satisfactory definite description of it, cannot account for the power and enchantment that drives the impulse to recollection. Rather, it is the logical source of that alienation intrinsic to recollection, the exclusionary difference of time present from

55. Ibid., 74.

56. First performed in Vienna in 1840, with its author playing the lead. As an original production of the Alt-Wiener Volkstheater, the comedy was broad, colloquial, and slapstick (Nestroy, "The Talisman," 15–92).

57. *Der Talisman* was itself in fact based upon an earlier, less successful, French farce of 1806, Dupeuty and de Courey's "Bonaventure" (ibid., 8).

58. Cf. Aristotle, *Physics* 219a.

time-that-was. So understood, the only way for an event to be related to the future is as a cause, but the total dissimilarity between past and present renders any such relationship essentially a fictional one. A necessary fiction perhaps, but one nonetheless, with devastating consequences for any philosophy of history.

The play has the effect it does because of the possibilities the text offers, and in this the text can reasonably be characterized as embodying the expectation of those possibilities. That is, the text exists, as it were, in anticipation of them. In *Repetition* Constantine Constantius attends several performances of *Der Talisman*, but only one of those, the first, is of the stuff to inspire recollection. The others are, in effect, nonevents, and it is to the event character of that first performance that we must look in order to understand how it, rather than its successors, reveals something of repetition. A first distinction to make is between the entire play as an event and the many separate events occurring in it, some of which may well in performance exceed any expectations we might have had of them from a simple reading of the text. A further distinction must also be made between the character of an event that makes it somehow "memorable" and the experience of beholding it that is the exclusive property of the event as a "Moment."[59] Thus there is on the one hand our beholding the actor who "comes walking," and on the other treasuring the memory of seeing him do that. The action and the beholding exist as one in the Moment, related to the text not historically but only as this particular realization of it. Further, the character of the Moment encompasses the beholder, not as an event with clearly drawn before-and-after demarcations but as the event of a person coming into existence in a new way, as Kierkegaard put it in the *Philosophical Fragments*, "not a change in essence but in being . . . a transition from not existing to existing."[60] Such a change, sharing in the uniqueness of the event, "looks forward," as he puts it, in that it bears its consequences within it. Like the performance of good deeds, in which Aristotle saw those who did them becoming better people, the Moment entails the future possibility of other moments. Into the *Dasein* of life, its colorless everydayness, the Moment makes a difference, creates a *différance*, "intervenes" in the interest of existence in the midst of what would otherwise be just history. The text provides the basis for the repetition that is the Moment, but the Moment keeps its own identity. The Moment anticipates other moments, but not

---

59. Deleuze calls this the "propitious moment" (*Difference*, 29).
60. Kierkegaard, *Philosophical Fragments*, 91.

as the result of historical research and reconstruction, but through what Aristotle thought of as *chance*, i.e., a state of affairs we did not create but certainly would have if the possibility had arisen.⁶¹

A Postmodern Paradigm

The text of 1 Corinthians 11:23–26, the basis of the liturgical use of those words, reports simply what they are and what their place is in the tradition. Part of a Pauline intervention in a situation where liturgical practice had gone astray, it contributes nothing new or unusual but, in terms of the concept of repetition, tells the Corinthians only something that they in fact already knew. It is not itself a liturgical event, but rather a disciplinary or doctrinal one, an epistolary intervention. The liturgical use of the text introduces new complexities, in that it repeats the words not as a report but in partial fulfillment of the very request that the text describes. The logical import of this is to render the liturgical use of the text entirely self-referential, in that it both repeats the request and fulfills it by so doing. And such a response of necessity constitutes precisely the sort of discrete, identifiable event anticipated by the text, something quite different from having merely recited the words. We can distinguish the liturgical use from aesthetic or dramatic uses, in that these latter are recitals for other purposes, whether to highlight the words' prophetic grandeur or to place them meaningfully in an instructional narrative. The entire purpose of liturgical use is, in contrast, by reason of its performative character to occasion a response that by its internal logic occurs as a distinct, Kierkegaardian, "Moment."

Keeping in mind that repetition is primarily a movement of thought rather than by definition a religious act, what was it about the comic theater that prompted Kierkegaard to set it higher than either the spectacle of opera or the seriousness of drama, to make it hint at the religious? After all, there is nothing beautiful or pleasing about farce, a literary form full of painful confusions, flawed characters, and ridiculous improbabilities. And any lessons it teaches are presented sufficiently tongue-in-cheek to rob them of any serious ethical intent.⁶² But the farce, like true religiousness, rejects the pleasures of the aesthetic and looks beyond the universally applicable recommendations of ethics. Where ethics warns against the sinful rejec-

---

61. Cf. Aristotle, *Physics* 195b–198a.

62. The most obvious lesson of *Der Talisman* is that there is nothing wrong with being red-headed.

tion of its standards, farce gleefully abandons them. Where neither beauty nor probity of action can occasion something like the Moment, farce can. Beauty and ethical responsibility each represent standards often applied to liturgical action, e.g., that it be an impressive foretaste of heaven, that we "participate" simply because we ought to, or because doing so will make us better people. As a genre, however, the gospels qualify not as tragedy with its familiar admonitions to avoid the same fate, but in the very least as comedy, happy ending courtesy of the Resurrection and the promise of eternal life for all. And what could *more* fly in the face of experience than the Resurrection, unless it be the declaration "This is my body"? The Moment in farce and the Moment in liturgy transcend alike the canons of beauty and the demands of propriety in a leap of faith that ever risks a fall into the pompous or the merely strange.

Again, if we take the liturgical use of the Eucharistic words as actually a Kierkegaardian repetition, a Moment, what demands does this place on the celebrant, the circumstances, and the audience of the liturgy? It does, after all, seem both unrealistic and unreasonable to expect that the Eucharistic ceremony must always evoke words as ecstatic as those of Kierkegaard upon his first viewing of *Der Talisman*. Does not the Moment represent precisely the sort of ideal unattainable in the present except through recollection?

The first consideration to take into account is that the Moment is not the achievement of any single individual but emerges rather from a complex of factors including time, place, and the character and mood of all present. Minimizing distractions and concentrating are, of course, to be commended, but acknowledging the liturgy as an opportunity rather than an ecclesial obligation hews closer to the point. Above all, it must be recognized that the celebration is a self-identical, unique event that, even though itself a repetition, cannot be repeated historically. It is its own one, last, best chance. Further, it is one of those milestones of life from which we grow forward, additively, as suggested long ago in Ignatius of Antioch's description of the Eucharist as "the medicine of immortality."[63] The faithful may indeed not celebrate the Eucharist with the Lord until he comes but will do it many times before then.[64] That there is still room for human limitation is self-evident, in that even simple recital can sometimes be an occasion for enlightenment, as in learning more of what a sentence means from having

---

63. Ignatius of Antioch, Letter to the Ephesians 20:2 in Staniforth and Louth, *The Apostolic Fathers*.

64. Lk 27:18, Mk 14:25, Mt 26:25, cf. *Didache* 10:60.

heard it said again. And many otherwise ancillary factors, some as humble as seeing the same faces and hearing the same greetings on a Sunday morning, can still qualify as a repetition, a Moment, even if a modest one.

Perhaps the most critical aspect of the Eucharistic words is their fundamentally social character in the Moment. The text is of its very nature a conventional artifact representing elementary agreement on issues as basic as orthography and the semantics of translation. Its canonicity is accepted, despite the critical issues raised by its absence from the Fourth Gospel, and accordingly positions it as the most central portion of worship. Its use is, particularly for Protestants, unfailingly public in execution but individually private and personal as a response to the request for remembrance. The worshipping community speaks in the person of the celebrant; it can only speak as an assemblage derivatively. Thus in the Eucharistic liturgy each and every one of those present worships, rather than merely participating in worship, the real point of the "priesthood of all believers." And it is this very complex social Moment, particularly the situation of the individual in that Moment, that exemplifies both the personal and the social reality of the Eucharistic words.

Returning to our initial concern about the fate of the Eucharistic text in the hands of its interpreters, it should be clear that the Eucharistic remembrance constitutes a single action that is its own fulfillment, and it is the fulfillment through repetition in the Moment that defines its meaning, over anything else. The only interpretive equivalent to it is not another text, but another Moment, with the caveat that no later Moment can reproduce any earlier one historically. This serves as a constant reminder to the biblical literalist that text is based on the physical realities of human communication and comes to its full power only in situations that are of their very nature social. Doctrines of literal inspiration deny the text the range of semantic content that belongs naturally to it as a social artifact, reducing it effectively to a semiotic marker. And claims of individual inspiration, intended to validate understandings of the text that are supposedly obvious to reasonable people, locate grace not in the complexities of the grace-filled Moment, but in the self-validating ruminations of Enlightenment rationalism. The questions raised by Plato in the *Phaedrus* also find their solution here, in that the meaning of the text is no longer what *was* said, but what *is* said, given that a historical recreation of the original utterance is neither fully possible nor in principle valid.

Beyond the Body

But no matter how effectively we have been able to separate the Eucharistic words from either literal historical-critical meanings, we cannot entirely escape the suggestion implicit in those words that something has actually *happened* because of them. It is to this that we must now turn.

4

WORD AND DEED

> [Words] are "signs" of things and have such power that they bring the speech of one absent to our ears without voice.
>
> —Isidore of Seville[1]

In Christian sacramental practice the Eucharist occurs as a temporally unique liturgical act that can on occasion extend over a greater span of time and place, as in the later distribution of the sacrament to those absent from the service for reasons of illness. The most central part of the Eucharistic "anaphora" begins with the "this" in "This is my body" and extends to its conclusion in the words of the *anamnesis*, the request or command that an action, likewise a "this," be done as a remembrance:

> ... the Lord Jesus on the night when he was betrayed took a loaf of bread, and when he had given thanks, he broke it and said, "This is my body that is for you. Do this in remembrance of me."
>
> In the same way he took the cup also, after supper, saying, "This cup is the new covenant in my blood. Do this, as often as you drink it, in remembrance of me."[2]

---

1. *Etymologies* I.3, quoted in Curtius, *European Literature*, 313.
2. 1 Cor 11: 23-25.

Beyond the Body

While the "this" in "this is" in Luke 22 and 1 Corinthians 11 appears to serve as a reference to a physical object, its counterpart in "do this" refers not to a physical object at all but rather to one event that at the time of utterance has just occurred and to another that may do so at some indeterminate time in the future. Referring assertions like "this is" belong to the sort of factual declarations that J. L. Austin dubbed "locutionary." "Do this," plainly not a declaration at all, is rather an example of more broadly intended communicative speech acts termed by Austin "illocutionary" or "perlocutionary," comprised in this case both by the act of making a request or command to be remembered, as well as the semantic content that specifies what is to be done.[3] The occurrence of such speech acts and their relative indifference to criteria of truth or falsity have long been known, though only rarely adverted to. Aristotle recognized them in *On Interpretation*, using prayer as an example (17a), but was content to relegate them to a future, largely unfulfilled, direct consideration as aspects of rhetoric and poetry. Augustine, drawing upon more highly developed Stoic discussions of logic and grammar, both identified a broader range of examples and pointed more accurately to their status as actions:

> For either a statement is made in such a way that it is held to be subject to truth or falsity, such as 'every man is walking' or 'every man is not walking' and others of this kind. Or a statement is made in such a way that, although it fully expresses what one had in mind, it cannot be affirmed or denied, as when we command, wish, curse, and the like.[4]

Such commonly used forms of speech that do not meet the requirements of being true or false but which still have meaning in that their very use accomplishes some intended purpose, Austin classed under the heading of "performative utterances." He proposed five broad classes of these, each with a distinctive name and description: 1) Utterances like "We hold these truths to be self evident . . . " he referred to as *verdictive*," in that they act to declare a judgment or a finding. 2) Uses that of themselves commit the speaker to a course of action, as in "promising," "proposing," "championing," and "giving one's word," belong to the general category of

---

3. Austin, *How to Do Things*, 1–11. Austin in fact refers to naïve object reference as a "descriptive fallacy." Cf. idem, "Performative Utterances" in *Philosophical Papers*, 234.

4. Augustine, *De dialectica*, 85; 123nn2–3. For the source of this reference, see the much fuller discussion of the relation of Augustine's logic and grammar to Stoic sources in Irvine, *Textual Culture*, 168–89.

commissive. 3) Austin further used *behabitive* for a behavioral subcategory of commissives exemplified in uses like "apologize," "welcome," "thank," and both "curse" and "bless." 4) Reprising the "syncategorematic" terms of late medieval logic, he labeled terms that move argument through its various stages without contributing to it semantically *expositive*: "I turn next to," "I quote," and "I repeat that." 5) Finally, terms like "naming," "urging," "ordering," "commanding," and "recommending" that encompass a wide spectrum of use where there is a strong element of advocacy he called *exercitive*. In place of truth or falsity of reference as criteria of validity, Austin advocated a standard of success or effectiveness indicated by the terms "happy" and "unhappy."[5]

We might, if we wished, make a preliminary case for taking the declarative "this is" in the Eucharistic anaphora as a performative of Austin's verdictive sort, but this will quickly be seen as a dead end. Simply naming something, after all, does not change what it is, although the act of so doing could for other reasons radically alter our relation to it.[6] Further, the purpose of a declaration may not be change at all, but simply to mark that the declaration itself has been made, e.g., "from this day forth . . . ." The request for remembrance in the closing words of the anaphora, on the other hand, clearly fulfills the requirements of performative language, in particular of the "exercitive" sort.[7] The conditions of the request, the "this," are basically met by both saying the words and doing concomitantly the physical actions the words indicate, i.e., taking bread and taking wine in the context of saying the complete text of the anaphora in a group act understood to be one of remembrance.

Austin's interest in the performative utterances found in "ordinary language" developed more or less contemporaneously with a recognition among formal logicians of the complexity of common speech. His fascination with the panoply of examples that can plausibly be called performative seems to have been stimulated particularly by the insight they provide into

---

5. Austin, *How to Do Things*, 147–63.

6. Ibid., 5.

7. We should not, however, overlook that there are other classes of performative uses among which "do this" might plausibly be included, as, for instance, "perlocutionary" uses of declarative utterances as hints or prompts to the hearer rather than commands, requests, or recommendations. "Do this" could well also function as one of Austin's "verdictives," declaring thereby that "*this*," rather than some other "*that*" is what should be done. And no great stretch is required to note the speaker's own potential *commitment* to doing "this" again, should the extent of life permit.

perfectly intelligible realms of speech that have little or nothing to do with formal logic and only accidental relevance to observational reference. His disinterest in searching out formal structures by which performative utterances might as a whole be reduced to a more comfortable uniformity is, I believe, fully justified by the unresolvable differences among them that closer examination reveals. This has to do on the one hand with logical or grammatical issues like the transitivity or intransitivity of the actions thus performed, and on the other with the dizzying diversity of effects that the circumstances of utterance can have on the nature, effectiveness, and temporal consequences of those actions.

The essentially descriptive approach to performatives Austin took stands in marked contrast to the more structuredly analytic work of John Searle that followed it, as well as to parallel developments in the new logical discipline of formal pragmatics.[8] Both these latter aimed to produce prescriptive criteria for the validity of performatives and other pragmatic

---

8. Formal philosophical convention assigns performative utterances like "do this" to a category of language use called "pragmatic." Where words are used to *refer*, semantic analysis looks for the conditions under which that is done, such that those references can be determined to be either true or false. Where they occur in sentences that *assert* their truth, syntactic analysis determines whether their claims were made in a grammatically intelligible way. Where sentences are used by a speaker to *communicate* something to a hearer or hearers, pragmatics both analyzes and critiques the language used as the instantiation (*realia*) of that communication. Attempts to formalize the language of science along the positivist lines set out in Russell and Whitehead's *Principia Mathematica* of 1927 had lost some of their aura of apodicticity when it came to light that the more popularly couched "verification principle" promulgated by A. J. Ayer in *Language, Truth and Logic* (1936) and *The Foundations of Empirical Knowledge* (1940) could not itself fulfill its own stated criteria for meaningfulness. Austin first addressed these difficulties in 1940 in lectures on "The Meaning of a Word," returning to them in a more direct critique of Ayer in lectures that later became *Sense and Sensibilia*. Perhaps the first formal acknowledgement of meaningful language use outside the bounds of empirical verification appeared in the widely used Hans Reichenbach *Elements of Symbolic Logic* (1947), a sizable section of which on the "Analysis of Conversational Language" included a very well-detailed discussion of logical terms "used in a pragmatic capacity." To classify such terms Reichenbach borrowed the "moods" of verbs familiar from traditional grammar, in this case the interrogative and the imperative. The absence of an "optative" mood in English, however, he took as license to overlook broader performative uses related to the imperative like "wish," "request," "beg," "pray," "plead," and so on. In the continuing literature on what is now generally considered under that heading, Robert Stalnaker's 1970 essay "Pragmatics" provides the most classic and enduring description of it as a field of logical inquiry and analysis. See Reichenbach, *Elements*, 251–354, esp. 336–44; Stalnaker, "Pragmatics," 272–89; Habermas, *Communication*, 1–68, *The Theory of Communicative Action*, 2 vols; Searle, *Social Construction*.

usages that would more narrowly approximate the truth-functional criteria governing ordinary declarative statements. For social theorists on the Continent, the so-called "linguistic turn" of postwar Anglo-American philosophy that this represented, exemplified in remarks that began "When *we* say that . . . ," hinted at an unacknowledged social dimension to "ordinary language" that promised to provide a window on the logical structure of social communication. The earliest, and perhaps most influential, effort to realize this potential was the "universal pragmatics" proposed by Jürgen Habermas in 1976, an effort that drew upon extensive international resources in several disciplines, including not only social theory but logic, Anglo-American philosophical analysis, and theoretical linguistics. This effort was considerably furthered in Habermas's two-volume work on the theory of communicative action (1981) and, ultimately, in Searle's *The Construction of Social Reality* (1995).

While the analyses of social action developed by Habermas and Searle are of inestimable value in uncovering the social dimensions of religious language, particularly in liturgical use, the claim of universality for them is less so. As mentioned earlier, far too much shoehorning of very disparate instances is required to support any claim of universality very comfortably. Further, given that, as Durkheim once observed, logic can expect only as much acceptance as society is willing to extend to it,[9] a universally applicable logic of social acts suffers at least the appearance of circularity. The problematic this describes is obvious: to make as much use as possible of the technical means for parsing, as it were, "do this" as a performative without losing sight of its particularity both as an expression and as an utterance. Further, what authority can we expect to claim for any results of such an analysis, given that very separately adjudicated religious doctrinal issues are legitimately implicated? My aim here is neither to demolish traditional doctrinal descriptions of Eucharistic belief like transubstantiation nor to tender any new candidates for that role, but to develop a persuasive account, rooted in a contemporary intelligibility, not of the doctrine, but of the belief itself.

---

9. "The value we attribute to science depends, in the last analysis, upon the idea we collectively have of its nature and role in life, which is to say that it expresses a state of opinion" (Durkheim, *Elementary Forms*, 439).

Beyond the Body

An Anatomy of Verbal Performance

Utterances qualify generally as speech acts, rather than simply as things said, by reason of their being events that create states of affairs where interpersonal relationships and behavioral expectations have been changed. They are semantically defined, even if trivially so, by the names we give them for what they do, e.g., a promise promises, a request requests, and so on. Synonyms for these names add a dimension of descriptive nuance, in that we may promise something by pledging or make a request by simply asking. The most general form for such speech acts shows a speaker as agent saying something that imposes upon a hearer or audience an obligation to act. It can be schematized in various ways, including that suggested by Habermas:

"I . . .   you that . . .   ."
 [verb]   [sentence][10]

This format also allows of phrasing in passive form, thereby masking the identity of the speaker or agent, as in "You are hereby instructed to . . . ." The speaker or agent, as well as the hearer or audience, can also be elided as understood, so that, for instance, "I ask you to do this" becomes "do this" without loss of speaker/hearer reference. Under certain conditions, speaker and hearer can be implied, but without specific identity: "It is wished that . . ." and "I name this ship . . . ," the latter a regulatory advisement to all current and future persons who may have occasion to refer on a formal basis to the object so named. It must be strongly noted, however, that under no circumstances does the identity of the speaker who is "I" vanish altogether. The speech act is inextricably tied to the speaker as agent, a key point for understanding the temporal reach of a speech act as an event. Although conceivable in the setting of a group recitation, "we" has no voice of its own that is other than that of the "I"s who comprise it.

Over and above not being a good fit for all cases, however, the reductionist elegance of such a schema does no justice at all to the potentially bewildering complexity of even the simplest speech acts.[11] Not wishing to

---

10. Habermas, *Communication*, 35. John Searle later formalized this more concisely as !↑W(H does A), wherein that a hearer H does an action A is the propositional content of a verbal act whose words express a wish for that to happen. Thus excising the speaker as agent allows for defining the speech act more verifiably in terms of its results. Searle, *Expression and Meaning*, 13–14.

11. Searle remarks that the complexity of such seemingly simple acts "would have

multiply intellectual entities needlessly, it seems clear that "speech act" as a term epitomizes rather than catalogs a complex of open variables ranging from the identity, intention, and transactional role of the speaker and any actual or potential hearers to the congeries of circumstances immediately shaping the act, its anticipated results, and the inevitable panoply of ambiguities inherent, as per Plato, in language. Considering these as the "requirements" for a speech act to have taken place, then: 1) any given such act summarizes or instantiates a set of presuppositions that together constitute what we will call its *situation* as an utterance;[12] 2) to be socially significant that utterance must occur in time as an *event* with consequences for either the speaker or any hearers, even potential ones; and 3) for the utterance to be intelligible to its hearer or hearers it must be both semantically and lexically effective, capable of taking the form of *text*. Though by no means precise equivalences, it should be noted that *situation* and the Kierkegaardian concept of the Moment are strongly interrelated, as are repetition and text. The event of utterance, on the other hand, pertains to both these while uniquely imparting a temporal dimension to the act. To each of these, situation, event, and text, we now turn.

Situation

Institutional setting, physical ambiance, social milieu, language conventions, social position, official role, authorization, familiarity, expectation, intention, anticipated effect, and response are all, with many more, possible elements of a speech-act situation and can determine the most comprehensive description of it, just as they may be considered to be pragmatically, if not semantically, presupposed by it.[13] Such presuppositions serve as keys, not completely available within the act itself, to understanding it.[14] Expec-

---

taken Kant's breath away, if he had ever bothered to think about such things" (*Social Construction*, 3).

12. Using here Austin's representation of such an event as "Speech-situation S_o," in "How to Talk: Some Simple Ways" in *Philosophical Papers*, 134.

13. Thus Stalnaker: "There is no conflict between the semantic and pragmatic concepts of presupposition: they are explications of related but different ideas.... To presuppose a proposition in the pragmatic sense is to take its truth for granted, and to assume that others involved in the context do the same" ("Pragmatics," 279).

14. These are Habermas's "conditions of possible understanding," meaning thereby the elements of a broader description of the act that purports to tell us what it is in the context of our general knowledge of the world at large. Habermas, *Communication*, 1.

tation and response in particular frame that act temporally in regard to its potential force, extent, and success.

Contrary to our innate belief that actions have readily discernible causes, the relationship between a speech act and the presupposed attitudes, facts, conventions, and so forth that shape it is by no means one of logical necessity. That someone be institutionally authorized to perform a certain speech act may be a necessary but is not of itself a sufficient condition for that act to be performed successfully, in that the person to whom the act is directed may not be able to legitimately accept either the obligation it imposes or the change in state that it would mandate. Presuppositions like physical ambiance, familiarity, or expectation, on the other hand, serve more as prompts to an action than formal enablers of it, despite the fact that the action may never have happened if, for instance, the weather, prior acquaintance, or the speaker's mood of the moment had been otherwise. These latter are such that we may even, if we wish, act in spite of them. Apparent in logic, if not in intuition, is that the relationship of such presuppositions to each other is one of juxtaposition rather than conjunction, i.e., we may not join these together for the purpose of constructing a "logical" chain of causes for action but must be content to see their influence on the action in accumulative or accretive terms.[15] Logical consequences can exist within any given presupposition, as that someone authorized to perform a particular speech action have some ritually obligatory piece of equipment to do so, but between the different pragmatic presuppositions of speech acts no mutual implication can exist. Acting altogether spontaneously, as though without presuppositions, honors this principle in the breach, in that spontaneous or "unpremeditated" action is nonetheless characterized as such by that condition.

Without doubt, the foremost formal determinant among the presuppositions of a speech act for its happiness or success is the status or role of the speaker. Only institutionally established judges or juries, for instance, can declare guilt or innocence. Only duly authorized persons can bestow academic degrees. Only someone with sufficient control over the circumstances of its fulfillment can issue a promise. Only one who understands the conditions of its accomplishment can make a valid request. All such take place within a social milieu made up of language, custom, law, and

---

15. Reichenbach considered the assertion of a proposition to be a pragmatic rather than a semantic use of language. Such assertions, therefore, could not be combined propositionally in any way that would enable logical entailment: "Juxtaposition, therefore, constitutes the pragmatic analogue of conjunction" (Reichenbach, *Elements*, 338–39).

their commonly related expectations. These establish the roles of both the speaker and hearer(s) within a social relationship such that obligations are incurred in both directions: the speaker "has the right" to expect acceptance, acquiescence, or compliance insofar as the act implicitly or explicitly calls for those. The hearer "has the right" to clarity and plausibility on the part of the speaker in performing the act and setting the conditions for whatever its fulfillment may be. The speaker's formal role provides in great measure the "force" of the act, but is at the same time the source of the hearer's corresponding role. The boundaries of both roles are clear, or at least clear enough that deliberate ambiguity, unreasonable criteria for compliance, upstaging, and role reversal are recognizable infringements. The primary movers for such behaviors are readily identifiable as political or social power and/or disaffection with such power.[16]

One pitfall we must especially avoid is to consider the speaker's intention in the utterance as a defining condition of it. Austin's example of a promise that was insincerely[17] made, raises the question of just how much or how little the "intention" of the speaker defines an act of performative language. A "false" promise, after all, "happy" or not, still counts as a promise, albeit an "insincere" one. The promisee, whose state of mind is equally relevant as a presupposition of the situation, is in any case free to believe or disbelieve in the speaker's sincerity. Neither the intention of the speaker nor the expectation of the promisee make this a promise, but the form of the words themselves. Thus while that form of words may classify a particular speech act as a promise and supply its assertoric content, viz., that there is something I say I will certainly do, it is the act of utterance itself, and the speaker's awareness in so doing that instantiates the promise. That act could not have come about if the speaker had not intended it, even though this intention is of course different from the 'one expressed in the speech act as it occurs. Locating something called the "intention" in all of this, something that is different from the form of words, is thus less simple than it might seem. Ordinary usage provides little help, tending as it does to regard "intent" and "intention" as synonyms, but adverbial uses of "intent" are by no means identical to either of these. "Her intention to communicate" says something rather different from "She was intent upon

---

16. Examples of the concept of power as evidenced in subjective interactions like those of which the liturgy of the Eucharist is comprised have been very persuasively described by Siobhán Garrigan in *Beyond Ritual*, 122–37.

17. Austin, *How to Do Things*, 109–10.

communicating" or "Her communicative intent was clear." The first may be a verbally expressible mental content, but the next two denote a quality of action or what is often called a "state of mind." When we consider that the speaker's intention might also have been to teach the hearer a lesson about trusting him, the role of intention in the speech act becomes murkier still.

Ordinary conversations abound, of course, in instances where A says something intending one thing and B hears something quite different from or reacts quite differently from what was expected. Naively construed, we should be able to get a handle on what is said by consulting or appealing to the "consciousness" of the speaker.[18] All B really needs to do if B is confused is to access A's consciousness through a well-phrased question or two, and A's intention in speaking, the identity of the perlocutionary act, would be clarified. But for several reasons this cannot succeed. One is that it sees language as producing a report or list of mental contents in translated form, independently perhaps of whether there may be any higher-level governing logical coherence to that list or not. This reporting is supposedly made possible by being able to access one's own thoughts in an act or experience of introspection referred to in saying "I looked into my own mind and saw that . . . ." The fault here is that, typical of what has been argued against as the "experiential-expressive" view of language,[19] the speaker's "original" intention as a mental content is a moving target, the identity of which has been irretrievably relativized by placement in the temporal sequence initiated by the questioner. Practically speaking, the questioner may in fact have introduced any number of variables into the situation that could serve to cloud or fracture the identity of the original utterance. The speaker may feel challenged by being questioned and could respond defensively, disdainfully, or even dismissively, each of which distinctly recharacterizes the original occurrence for purposes of further discussion.

Trying to identify an event by an appeal to the speaker's "intention" falls prey to the sort of psychological fallacy that equates the meanings of words with the mental state of the speaker, quite independently of the words of the speech act itself. This relativizing of verbal meaning according to mental states easily reinforces the idiosyncratic emotional meanings of statements while unacceptably trivializing their conceptual content. It also suggests that meaning can only have been successfully conveyed once

---

18. Appeal to "consciousness" as a source of definitive meaning is found in Hirsch, *Validity*, where it, however applies primarily to determining meaning in *written* texts.

19. Lindbeck, *Nature of Doctrine*, 31–45.

the hearer has the same mental content as the speaker and can enjoy the possibility of repeating exactly the same words, with the same "intention," to someone else. But this is to raise the specter of an emotional Donatism, where only those with the proper feeling for what has been said can participate successfully in discussion, and where those lacking those feelings or having different ones must of necessity be excluded from it.

For performative speech acts like promises or requests, therefore, the intention of the speaker cannot be the sole guarantor of meaning. Assuredly it broadens the basis on which we can interpret or understand the act, but it also uncovers thereby a breadth of possibilities that all too easily trails off into a meaningless relativism. Any hope we have to learn the meaning of the speech act must begin and remain with the form of words itself, although this too is likewise the result of extensive social interaction and cultural development.

Event

Again, we use "speech act" to refer to that aspect of a particular utterance that has communicative purpose and intended effect. That such an act is "performative" distinguishes it as accomplishing or attempting to accomplish that purpose through its very being said. The various types of performatives discerned by Austin—verdictive, behabitive, commissive, and so on—reflect different situations of social or institutional use and their correspondingly different potential criteria for "happiness" or "unhappiness," success or failure. The complexities of each such situation, the "facts" so to speak that comprise it, frame the speech act by being what it is that is "the case" when the utterance takes place, echoing intentionally here the opening line of Wittgenstein's *Tractatus*.[20] As facts from the worlds of nature, society, and the speaker's inner life these make up what we may well call the "lifeworld" of the utterance, i.e., the physical, social, and psychological space in which it occurs.[21] In that lifeworld the utterance constitutes not

---

20. "The world is all that is the case" (Wittgenstein, *Tractatus*, 6–7).

21. Habermas's description of these three "worlds" in "What is a Universal Pragmatics," 67–68, prefigured his wholesale adoption of the concept of "lifeworld" in *Theory of Communicative Action*. In the first volume of the latter work he refers to it definingly as "the correlate of processes of understanding," "formed from more or less diffuse, always unproblematic, background convictions," and "a source of situation definitions that are presupposed by participants as unproblematic" (*Theory of Communicative Action*, 1:70).

simply a momentary speech act, but an "event" that creates and anticipates consequences over time.

Calling a speech act an event, however, is not without difficulties. For one thing, the logical tradition since Aristotle has been firmly reductionistic in classifying events as denumerable points in a continuity of motion and change primarily concerned with physical objects.[22] Very summarily described, this consists in limiting events to single instances where causes bring about an alteration from a potential to an actual state of affairs that is nonidentical with its predecessor. The locus of the change in the continuity of time can be referred to as "now," as in the sentence "It is happening now." The state of rest that results at the conclusion of the change can also be classified as a "now," although perhaps more commonly understood in spatial terms, as in "It is here now," denoting both the completion of a physical motion and the resulting existence of an object in a given state. Aristotle recognizes events of larger temporal and less specifically perceptual scope, although in passing and rather dismissively on the grounds that they lack the immediacy of "now," saying "we do not speak so of the Trojan war or Deucalion's flood; though time is continuous between us and these events, they are not near."[23] Although some types or classes of performative speech acts can indeed be related to physical objects and actions, as in "I order you to close the door," others certainly cannot: "I hold these truths to be self-evident." Donald Davidson, in a classic essay on events, solves this by enlarging the class of objects in general to include events by treating "I apologize" not as a performative utterance but as the description of an event that becomes an "entity" simply by being what it is, viz., apologizing.[24]

A second, and more serious, difficulty implicit in this position concerns the relationship of events broadly separated from each other by time. An Aristotelian event occurs in a "now" that is bounded on either side, as it were, by a "before" and an "after."[25] Insofar as time can be treated analo-

---

22. Aristotle's assessment of events in *Physics*, V bears this out, despite his attempt to broaden the scope of kinds of events to include qualitative as well as quantitative changes. His chosen example, personal health, however, pertains nonetheless to qualities of a physical body. Aristotle, *Physics* 224a. The durability of this point of view is amply illustrated by Donald Davidsons' statement: "most events are understood as changes in a more or less permanent object of substance" (Davidson, "Individuation," 302).

23. Aristotle, *Physics* 223a.

24. Davidson, "Individuation," 296.

25. Perhaps best illustrated by the example ubiquitous to modern discussions, the event of Caesar's death at the hand of Brutus. See Pianesi and Varzi, "Events," 3–48.

gously to spatial continuity, we can therefore specify temporal coordinates for that "now," regardless of whether it happened in the past or is yet to come. Such a form of dead reckoning works well enough for practical purposes but loses some of its certainty when we consider that "now" is also simply a line that separates past from future, something that vanishes into the past as it simultaneously becomes what was to be (*Physics* IV.10; 218a). This evanescence of the present likewise raises ontological questions about both past and future, in that the former clearly no longer exists while the latter does not yet do so (*Physics* IV, 10; 217b). As it happens, the ultimate Aristotelian solution to reliably describing events in the face of such temporal ephemerality has already been supplied by the doctrine of the four causes—material, efficient, formal, and final (*Physics* II.3; 194b-195a). The result will be an infinite and eternal universe where time is the measure of motions (events) brought about in succession by their causes, including especially among these the prime, unmoved, mover of *Physics* VIII.5. Relations between events will be a matter largely of contiguity, suggesting more the terminal immediacy of the billiard table than the complexity of narrated experience. This leaves us on the one hand with the implausibility of everything in experience being the most recent effects of a traceable succession of causes that stops short of, but for practical purposes, not *far* short of infinity. On the other hand it clearly fails to account for any situational relationship where something like potential, or even actual, long-term influence is at stake. The situation of effects as themselves potential causes is left unprovided for, particularly where considerable temporal distance may in fact be the case as with the Trojan War above.

Interest in the challenge that events pose for both logic and ontology has also, however, arisen quite outside the formal tradition that characterizes them primarily as instances of cause and effect. In *Being and Event* and its recent successor, *Logics of Worlds*,[26] Alain Badiou proposed an ontology of events modeled on developments in set theory, one surprisingly reminiscent of the Platonizing tendencies of early twentieth-century mathematics. The difference between 1 and 0 of itself depicts the difference between a) that which exists in that it can be counted-as-one and b) that, which has no right even to be referred to as "that," which cannot. The contrast is thus not between something that exists and the same thing said simply not to exist, but between something that can be counted —perhaps named—and what Badiou terms "the Void." We can see this likewise as the difference between

---

26. Badiou, *Being and Event* and idem, *Logics of Worlds*.

"something" and "nothing" or, more pointedly, the difference between a recognized state of affairs and utter emptiness. If a set specifically defined by its members has no members, statements made about that set will be meaningless rather than false.

Statements about events, like statements about sets, assume a multiple of elements configured together in what Badiou refers to as a "situation," much as Austin subsumes setting, the speaker's qualifications, the appropriateness of the audience, and potential consequences as constitutive of a "speech-situation." In the case that these elements remain unremarked individually but nonetheless are considered collectively as a singularity, Badiou's term "evental site" points up the absence of a logical or ontological connection between those elements and the external effort required to name or otherwise identify the site as that of an event. That there must be some connection or consistency between the elements and the name of the event, without which that name would be void, is recognized by introducing the evaluative standard, rooted in human interpersonal experience, of "fidelity."[27] Where orthodoxy evaluates the logical consistency of a given statement with prior spoken or written exemplars, fidelity considers only completeness of what is given of the event in its appearance or "presentation."

The void for Badiou must not be understood as a generalized nothing or absence of a particular existence, but rather as whatever stands opposite the singularity that can be named an event. The presuppositions or elements of a situation are not singularities in their own right but rather part of the great multiple that is what the world routinely, "naturally," or "normally" is. To be an event, a collection of these must constitute a singularity and be named as such in an "intervention" that would, using Austen's terms, be itself a performative action of either the verdictive or exercitive sort. Events, thus, are neither normal nor natural, standing rather in contrast to both custom and expectation. In keeping with Badiou's latter-day Marxism, events change states of affairs in ways that are recognized and therefore deserve the appellation historical. They represent the emergence of the new, the challenging, and the different over against the perdurance of the natural, the normal, or the neutral.[28]

27. Badiou, *Being and Event*, 211, 507–8.

28. As Badiou defines these in the dictionary of terms he appends to *Being and Event*, 515–16

Word and Deed

The temporal "reach," so to speak, of a performative utterance as a speech event can vary greatly depending at least in part on the temporal durability of its presuppositions. Naming a ship, Austin's classic example, enjoins behavior even upon persons temporally far removed from the verbal act that is the christening, first of all so long as anything continues to exist that corresponds to the object named. Thus, bills of lading, itineraries, certificates of ownership, insurances, are governed over time by the legal obligation to use that name as an identifier. The absence of any remaining physical traces will still, however, leave untouched the obligation of, say, the historian to refer to that former object in a manner consonant with or faithful to the description given at the time of naming. Maintaining a consciousness of that obligation and fulfilling its conditions requires, as Badiou puts it, a "discipline" of time embodied not in the criteria of comparison so beloved of orthodoxy, but in a procedure that continues to recognize in the consequences of the original event what its presuppositions were. This procedure, this discipline of "fidelity"[29] endures so long as there are consequences that require it, but without formal limit on the length of time that might be involved.

Performatives that make a specific request, as the Eucharistic anamnesis does, bring more clearly into focus the role that presuppositions have in delineating the conditions under which a response to a request can be successful or not. In this regard, not only do we need to know that the requester is entitled to make a request and whether doing so is entirely reasonable or appropriate, but also who, even generically, are the person or persons to whom it is made, whether they constitute an appropriate audience for it in terms of their connection to the speaker, and whether they in fact have the ability to respond by fulfilling the conditions of what implicitly has been asked of them. In contrast to the situation of the historian, where fidelity comprises a recognition over time of the legal consequences of a specific act of naming, the request puts in place a state of affairs that imposes an obligation on its hearer or hearers, regardless of when it is heard, to do what has been asked. The class of appropriate hearers may be so locally narrow that the obligation to respond might have very little historical scope, or it could be so broadly or generically defined as to guarantee an obligation and a validity of response over a distance of time from the original request that is in principle undelimitable. Under the latter condition, we might well

---

29. See *Being and Event*, 211 on the "discipline" of time as foundation for an adequate understanding of an event in terms of its consequences.

speak of the normal passage of time as "transcended"[30] by both the request and its concomitant obligation to respond.

In regard to the manner of requesting, it is important to note that requests may be made in person, that is, where one person directly addresses another or others, all of whom are present to each other in a speaking situation, asking that something be done specifically by those addressed. Where, however, those addressed are generically defined as a class of those, for example, having membership in a defined group, it is clear that the request can reach an audience well beyond those present at the time of the original utterance. And in such situations it is likewise entirely plausible that the request be recognized as contained in a written document agreed upon by the group as providing an accurate account of its wording. Although learning of the request by such means may be once- or twice-removed from the speech-act situation in which it was made, it remains nonetheless a request by that speaker and none other, and responding to it can in no wise be construed as a response to anyone else, including others in the group. In this sense, any response to an original request will be first-order in its relationship to the speaker/requester, regardless of any temporal distance that may separate the two.

A situation that has, so to speak, "won" recognition as an event is no longer "normal" or "neutral," but is the result of an "intervention" in the normal process of things that thereby places it in the larger framework of the "world" in which it has been recognized. As such, it enables us to think of that world as a singularity related to, but exclusive of, all other possible worlds. Although Badiou's portrayal of situations, events, and points applies most basically to events initiated in sense perceptions, he does not exclude the possibility of what we customarily think of as "historic" events being points in the transcendental continuity of a world. In a discussion of Pascal that we will later return to, Badiou sketches a structure of belief that reflects his understanding of the relationship of events and world over time:

> . . . in Christianity and in it alone it is said that the essence of truth supposes the evental ultra-one, and that relating to truth is not a matter of contemplation—or immobile knowledge—but of intervention. For at the heart of Christianity there is that event— situated, exemplary—that is the death of the son of God on the

---

30. Using "transcends" here to note both that the realized consequences of an event comprise a greater time than that of the original event itself, and likewise that naming the event and its effect evoke "the infinite totality" of the "world" in which these occur. Badiou, *Logics of Worlds*, 591.

cross. By the same token, belief does not relate centrally to the being-one of God, to his infinite power; its interventional kernel is rather the constitution of the meaning of that death, and the organization of a fidelity to that meaning. As Pascal says, 'Except in Jesus Christ, we do not know the meaning of our life, or death, or god, or ourselves.'[31]

But where the consequences of the event of the death on the cross follow only logically for the believer from intellectually accepting the ontological claim that Jesus was the son of God, responding to his request to be remembered is to touch the person he was.

Text

Without words, even if only implied through gesture, there can be no speech act. A performative utterance has what we can call a "text" in the same sense that the words of a song as it is performed constitute the *text* of the song. Literary critical thinking has long assumed that text is something, recognized canonically in its written form, that harbors as if through containment, the meaning of the words of which it is comprised, the intent of their author, or a stable structure of intellectual catalysts that prompt the reader (or hearer) to assign or attribute a meaning to them. Each of these critical procedures, of course, provides some measure of satisfaction to one who asks what the text "means," but always with the proviso that this will depend upon factors quite outside it, factors like the lexical history of the words, the state of mind of their author at a particular point of personal history, and the random sophistication or accidental receptiveness of a given reader or hearer. But the words of the text in a performative utterance function not as what it may be thought to contain, but as yet another of its presuppositions. We note this odd relationship of text to event in sentences like "She said all there was to say." Text, to use Badiou's terms, appears only in its presentation, the one place where it participates in being counted as one, i.e., in an event. We can agree, therefore, with the proposition that "text" as the term most often is meant can in this sense at least be said not to "exist."

Text plays a critical role in a performative utterance like "do this" in that it is the form of the words in the utterance that allows us to recognize it as, e.g., command, order, or request. While that recognition can be thought

---

31. Badiou, *Being and Event*, 212.

of as an act of understanding, it is an understanding operating exclusively at the behest of cultural norms that in effect "intervene" to provide the criteria that determine what sort of language use has occurred. That there be an intervention is critical in that without a judgment external to the utterance, the text of it amounts to no more than a collection of sounds or signs assembled according to the way such things are ordinarily or "normally" done.[32] The text will be senseless where the hearer or reader cannot learn from it what objects or actions are referred to, or whether these are congruent with each other in describing what would, again ordinarily or normally, be expected in a situation presented in an event. The most extreme case of failure to meet normal semantic and/or lexical criteria in language use is epitomized in the so-called "category mistake," but it should be clear that the linguistic prehistory of the words in any text can easily provide ample scope for the nuance and ambiguity that are the daily bread of literary critical and philosophical enterprise.

Despite its disputable status as an existent, we can go back to, appeal to, argue the integrity of, correct, reread, rehearse, and replay text, activities that can be engaged in as many times as we wish or as opportunity offers. The challenge and threat that this represents is that novelty wears off, that is, the recurrence of an event leads away from rather than reinforces its status as innovative. The oft-repeated text becomes, over time, the normal, the natural, the ordinary, just as use-tested legal phrases and clauses become "boilerplate." If text is one of the necessary presuppositions of a speech act, how can the constant reuse of a text not negate any innovative effect we might want that use to achieve?

An interesting distinction emerges here between the repeating and the recurring. The Kierkegaardian caution that the founding events of faith cannot be repeated historically in any way that would enable the believer to experience them as though present at the time leaves untouched the phenomenon, familiar in daily life, of things that simply happen again. Difficulties of a mechanical sort, for instance, can reoccur any number of times, or at least as many as we have the patience for, until the source of the problem has been identified and remedied. The collective of occurrences, described individually in phrases like "the same thing happened again" becomes the presupposition for the event of our admitting that the

---

32. As Augustine put it, "But if I ask how the name of Aeneas is spelt, anyone who has learned to read will give me the right answer, based on the agreed convention which fixed the alphabet for all of us" (*Confessions* 1.13).

device has indeed "broken down." The same set of occurrences terminated by successful functioning, on the other hand, can lead to the distinct and very gratifying event of the resumption of normal operation. Even here, however, the possibility remains for it to be said that the problem had been resolved "just like last time."

The recurrence of text in situations of use is most often indicated by quotation marks. Recalling that Austen also considered "I quote" to be a performative, specifically of the "expositive" sort, makes it easier to recognize that our expectations of accuracy in quotation are conventional rather than logical. Quotations are neither true nor false, although attributions of authorship may indeed be so. *Mis*quoting occurs when conventional expectations of accuracy fail to be met, in that words may be either present or missing from the text that make this, in effect, a different text. The qualifying phrase "in effect" indicates that allegations of difference are raised by readers or hearers of the text, among whom the original author may also be numbered. The absence or alteration of a single word may, or may not, be occasion for a difference to be claimed, providing the most minimal, yet by no means the most insignificant, basis for claiming difference.[33] Misquoting also occurs when, despite the accuracy of the words provided, other portions of text that qualify the quotation significantly are absent. This is the most common reason given for claims of quotation-out-of-context, but in practical terms it points only to a mistake, deliberate or otherwise, of the quoter to recognize the real boundaries of the text. Just how much alteration constitutes a recognizable misquoting is a problem of intellectual rather than quantitative difference, that is, one that can only be resolved in a higher level of discourse. Gilles Deleuze, for whom difference rather than identity is the categorical basis of knowledge, distinguishes between material and conceptual differences when considering the problem of when successive iterations of text, or event, can properly be said to be repetitions in the sense of that term first suggested by Kierkegaard. Using Deleuze's terms, we can say at least provisionally that a material difference between original and quoted text will be significant only insofar as readers or hearers will refuse to accept the quoted text as conceptually congruent with the original.[34]

---

33. As in the case of the "Wicked" Bible of 1631, which lacked the "not" of the commandment against adultery. See Eisenstein, *Printing Press*, 81.

34. Deleuze, *Difference*, 270.

Beyond the Body

The most critical issue about recurring text, however, is not quotational accuracy but the seeming propensity of a given text to be read or presented in unique, innovative post-authorial performances, events that transcend the simple recurrence of the words, events of the sort described by Alain Badiou. In chapter three above we considered Kierkegaard's posed frustration in *Repetition* over the unrecoverable experience of a brilliant production of an otherwise quite forgettable Viennese farce and the emphasis this enabled him to place on the seeming paradox that the mere repetition of a text could occasion a dramatic moment of life-altering effect. But where *Repetition* showcased the difficulties of repetition, *Fear and Trembling*, published as it happens on the same day, demonstrated how it is that true repetitions can indeed come about.

The epigraph to Kierkegaard's *Fear and Trembling*, a quotation from Hamann, the enigmatic and unpredictable "Magus of the North" of Königsberg, describes a situation where what began as a seemingly simple gesture by Tarquin, one of the kings of Rome in the age before the Republic, achieved its fullness only when "read," as it were, by the person to whom it was actually addressed.[35] Although more readily understood as an admonition to the reader to have ears to hear,[36] the preface that follows raises a more subtle question about the relationship between the original gesture and its corresponding realization. In it Descartes, "a venerable, humble, honest thinker" comes in for lavish praise on the grounds that, unlike Kierkegaard's contemporaries, he refused to "go further" than the unquestionable root of human thought to which systematic doubt had led him. What this going further seems to have meant in a larger context for Kierkegaard was the attempt by means of critical tools ("mediation") to produce a new, higher, more comfortable meaning of a text than the original. He takes this up later in a lengthy consideration of Luke 14:26, where the followers of

---

35. As given in Livy, the story is that Sextus, son of Tarquin the Proud, having insinuated himself into the ranks of the neighboring, hostile Gabii, sent a messenger back to his father asking for orders on what to do next. Tarquin, rather than saying anything at all, simply wandered through his garden, casually beheading poppy plants of their blossoms with his stick. The messenger, frustrated by a lack of verbal response, returned to Sextus able to say only that his father had said nothing. Sextus, however, recognized in Tarquin's actions the order that he should eliminate the principal leaders of the Gabii, which he proceeded to do as quickly as possible. Kierkegaard's choice of a passage in Hamann to convey this tale treats Tarquin's gesture as an example of a speech act: "Was Tarquinius Superbus in seinem garten mit den Mohnköpfen *sprach* . . . ." (Kierkegaard, *Fear and Trembling*, i, 341, italics mine).

36. Mt 11:15, Mk 4:9, Lk 8:8.

Jesus are told they must "hate" their families if they are truly to become disciples. For Kierkegaard, nothing less than "hate," the literal text, will do.[37]

Neither Tarquin's son Sextus nor Descartes needed a method of decoding or a hermeneutical apparatus to understand what was required of them. Similarly, those who hear the injunction to "hate" know how they are to act, conditioned presumably as well, however, by the command in Luke 5:43–44 to love both neighbors and enemies. In short, the literal text is the basis or benchmark for further thought, but only such thought as comes in direct response to the text rather than as the result of applying an exegetical or philosophical template to it. The epitome of this process is the succession of stories of Abraham in the opening section of *Fear and Trembling* that Kierkegaard titles the "Exordium," or declaration of structural principles. Each story is completely faithful to the content of Genesis 22:1–2 as quoted, as well as the remainder of the text of that chapter. Each, however, succeeds in maintaining that fidelity while describing, in succession, a deception by Abraham of his son to save the latter's trust in God (I), Abraham's lifelong and debilitating disappointment in God for having required him to sacrifice his son (II), Abraham's unresolvable moral guilt over having been willing to kill Isaac (III), and Isaac's loss of faith at having seen Abraham's willingness to compromise his duties as a parent at the behest of God (IV).[38] Each of these tellings is entirely new, yet each remains the story of Abraham's trial. Each repeats the text implicitly, without changing any of the details given in it, but each is certainly a separate, unique event in the telling. Each embodies to some degree the aesthetic, ethical, and religious categories of response that are the concern of *Fear and Trembling* as a whole. The text of Genesis 22 counts as a presupposition of each telling, but in no way is any of them a logical consequence of it. In these properly so-called repetitions of the text new readings of the Abraham story are realized without loss of the original. Each counts as a Badiou event.

The occasioning of such repetitions is for Kierkegaard first of all the function of the poet who, however, can do no more than hold Abraham in awe as a hero. The truth is that the work of the poet, for all its romantic glamour, is simply work. The pastor who adopts conventional "mediating" interpretations of Abraham's story for use in sermons, e.g., that Abraham so loved God that he "was willing to offer him the best," is going further than the text, but merely by borrowing clichés that happen, like goods on a store

---

37. Kierkegaard, *Fear and Trembling*, 72–73.
38. Ibid., 10–14.

shelf, to have been ready to hand.[39] From borrowing like this no good can come.[40] The work required is the work of the poet, the maker, the writer, but with no guarantee of the results. The paradox of the moment of writing is that something new be the intended result, one of the quite literally infinite possibilities that the original text can presuppose. The necessary, though not sufficient, condition for this to happen is the "movement of faith."[41]

The Last Supper

When we consider the pragmatic, nonimplicative, relationship between event and presupposition, it becomes clear that the factors comprising the situation that occasions an event are very little governed by either logical or historical criteria. Further, even the notion that some presuppositions might be more "influential" for defining the event than others fails on the grounds that such influence would of necessity be restricted to psychological states of both the speaker and the hearer that are perforce not reliably available to us. On the one hand this seems self defeating, disallowing as it does the possibility of satisfyingly determining one of those presuppositions to be the defining or identifying factor of the event. On the other hand, however, it frees us from the limitations inherent in any single explanation and more than amply demonstrates why multiple characterizations and interpretations of events inevitably occur. It is precisely this indeterminacy of the relationship of situation to event that gives events, as it does literature, a wealth of possibilities for understanding.

The presuppositions that contribute most obviously to the situation of the Last Supper event have been clearly identified in the classic critical literature on the subject.[42] These include, for instance, that the supper likely was, regardless of the difficulties represented by the Joannine account, a Passover meal. Intrinsic to that characterization are the remembrance of historic deliverance, the words and actions of the ritual, the position of the speaker of those words as paterfamilias, the role of those present as participants, and the expectation that the ritual is itself a functional part of

---

39. Ibid., 28.

40. As illustrated by the case of the parishioner who decides to take the life of his own son in order to emulate Abraham. Ibid., 29.

41. Ibid., 34–36.

42 These include both Jeremias, *Eucharistic Words* and Conzelmann, *1 Corinthians*, 192–202 on 1 Cor 11:17–34.

the continuing history of Israel's deliverance. That the ritual was here being performed in Jerusalem reinforces its solemnity through appropriateness of place and raises it from private, individual significance to one of historic participation in its subject.

These are, however, not the only possible presuppositions to consider. For one thing, through its very dispersion, the Judaism of the period was a world religion for which ritual sacrifice in the temple at Jerusalem had become geographically distant. More problematically, the practice of sacrifice throughout the Roman religious world was so ubiquitous as to diminish its meaning as a distinguishing factor among religions. In short, the Passover meal at the time was ideally positioned to act as a locus of opportunity for experiment and innovation in regard to the concept of sacrifice.

There is more to be said as well about the complex character of Jesus as the speaker in the Last Supper ritual. Was he the seeker who subjected himself to John's baptism, the miracle worker of Galilee, the transfigured companion of Moses and Elijah in Mt 17:1–9 and Mk 9:2–10, the trenchant critic of the religious elite, or the tireless spinner of puzzles and parables in the synoptics? Each of these has seen use at some time or another as a vehicle of interpretation for either the person or his mission. But although as presuppositions of a request to be remembered each and all of these properly bear equal weight in portraying the man, there is some point to drawing special attention to the Jesus of the parables as a person quite often wont to beguile or bedazzle his followers with utterances enigmatic enough seemingly to defy even his own efforts at illumination. It should come as no surprise, therefore, that those present at the supper may have been no less baffled by the words of institution or interpretation over the bread and wine than have been followers in later ages.[43] Whether we regard these words, or those of the parables, as esotericisms open to private explanation as in Mk 4:33, *moralia* that never fail to provide lessons for life, or social conventions reflecting the character of the age rather than the challenging content of the words, the implicit assumption remains that those words are, on the face of it, not readily intelligible. The burden of understanding the supper falls, therefore, not on the words of institution but on the request to be remembered by means of their being said once again with ritual intention.

Lastly in regard to the elements of the Last Supper situation, the words of Jesus were spoken in neither church nor temple, but at a supper where his role was that of *primus inter pares*, the human leader of the group, not

---

43. Jeremias, *Eucharistic Words*, 164.

a visiting divinity. The description of the supper in John 13 points this up quite forcibly, whether or not it lacks the words of institution, may or may not have been a Passover meal, or has other, very different, purposes in mind.

Although it may seem prima facie that the crowning event in the Last Supper narrative is a transformation of the elements occasioned by the words "This is my body," the view of events suggested here points, again, not to those words but rather to the request for remembrance as the event per se. The prima facie evidence referred to is, of course, the very strangeness of the words of institution, implicitly rendering possible as they do a range of shocking implications from the mistaken, the self-deluded, or the magical to the anthropophagous.[44] Were events to be understood only as the strikingly odd or unusual, a resolute focus on those words as transformational would be more than justified. But when we ask further what actual consequences those words might have, considering that the situations that comprise events must not only appear in the world but somehow alter it, the balance of evidence changes. The only transformation that could occur is one without discernible consequences, despite the seemingly magical effects often imputed to Paul's words in 1 Cor 11:27–31 regarding those who commune unworthily.[45] There is, of course, the argument to be accounted for that the effect on the recipient is spiritual rather than material, but this reprises the unacceptable position of Ratramnus, for whom the Eucharistic presence, though figurative rather than physical, must yet effect sacramental change.

It was in fact the performative speech act, the use of the words, that properly constituted the event. As either a request or a command to its hearers, it created a state of affairs requiring a response to be made on a

---

44. Possibilities alluded to by Augustine in considering Jn 6:54, "Except you eat," He says, "the flesh of the Son of man and drink his blood, you shall not have life in you." Augustine notes that in saying this Jesus "seems to commend a crime or vice." His solution to the problem is to insist the words are meant figuratively rather than literally. Augustine, *On Christian Doctrine* 3.16.

45 Although from a comparative-religious perspective the punishment of those who partake unworthily of the body must necessarily be the magical act of a sacred object that has been profaned, broader scholarly opinion notes that it is the *sin* of partaking unworthily that merits punishment. Further, that sin is properly not against the elements themselves but against the community as body of Christ, the unity of which is wounded by the communicant's failure in "discernment" (*diakrinein*). For support of this broader view see: Murphy-O'Connor, *Keys*, 216; Keener, *1-2 Corinthians*, 99; Conzelmann, *1 Corinthians*, 202–3.

continuing basis in an entirely indefinite future, not once but many times. Requests and commands, like many of the other performatives Austin describes, can be cast in the passive voice and thus do not necessarily imply their issuance by a particular person, as in cases like "It is hereby requested that," where the request would likely have been made by a property holder, civil authority, etc. But the request by the Jesus of the Last Supper clearly identifies that it is his own, personal, request and none other, thereby assuring that any post-event responses are necessarily indexed exclusively to it. The appropriateness or "happiness" of any such responses would be determined first by that reference to the original request and none other, and further by their fulfillment of its contents, viz., the recitation of the words and performance of the actions described in the anaphora, criteria that hue very close to the completeness of presentation or "fidelity" that Badiou attributes to responses to events.

The status of the request as an event is further enhanced by several factors. Although the words of interpretation over the bread and wine have no perceivable physical effect, their very difference from the norm for such words marks them as interventionary. While suggesting that objects could be transformed into other sorts of objects was within the bounds of the predictable in the ancient world,[46] breaking from the traditional words of interpretation was not. The same is true for the recasting of the concept of temple sacrifice into one of personal, redemptive death. Lastly, the self-reflexive structure of the request cannot be ignored. It is "this," i.e., the entirety of the anaphora, that it is requested be done, including both the words of interpretation and the statement of the request itself. It is specifically "this" that it is asked to be done, not a "that" referring to only the preceding actions and words. It is further in the nature of a request as a performative event that engendering the expectation of a response and the actions intrinsic to that response are effects that become part of the lifeworld of the hearer/responder, in that requests commonly seek to change the state of affairs from what it was to the state that will result from their fulfillment. Requests, however limited or humble, change things, if only by reason of their having been uttered. They function, at least minimally, on an *ex opere operato* basis.

The text of the Last Supper account stands as its most critical presupposition, since without the words of the request there would be no

---

46. Robert M. Grant notes several different sorts of such transformations, including both water into wine and wine into blood (*Miracle and Natural Law*, 95, 211–13).

performative utterance, no projected response, and no event. There is some question whether the request, found in Luke and 1 Corinthians as part of the so-called "long form"[47] of the anaphora but not in either Mark or Matthew, is an addition to some primitive *ur*-account of the supper or is itself the primary representative of the earliest tradition. But given the generally accepted position that the authentic Pauline letters predate the Synoptics, as well as the equally obvious preference of the liturgical tradition for including the request in the anaphora, it seems reasonable to assume that the request was generally believed to have been actually made by Jesus. In any event, the response of the historical church in continuing to celebrate the Eucharist, albeit reframed within the service of hymns and readings taken over from synagogue Judaism, indicates an understanding of the request as self-reflective of the performative act itself, rather than as either a commemorative funerary celebration,[48] a customary community supper resembling the Last Supper in John and 1 Corinthians, or a retrospectively restructured annual Passover meal. More simply put, the change in the state of affairs from that of an annual ritual observance to one of weekly or even daily frequency seems somewhat more plausibly the result of response to a request than of, for instance, the result of the early church creating innovative liturgical opportunities in the interests of promoting its own emerging organizational structure.

The text *tout simple*, then, is what was heard by those present at the Last Supper, first of all exclusive of context, language, interpretation, or their prior experiences of the speaking style of Jesus. As text, saving the unusual phrasing of the words of interpretation over the bread and wine and the request that this be done again in the future as an act of remembrance, it would have been familiar to them as the spoken part of the Passover ritual. Without the oddity of those words, however, this would have been an entirely normal reuse of the Passover ritual text in a completely natural situation, by no means the makings of an event of far-reaching consequence. It is the interventionary phrasing of the words, particularly in the request, that their use becomes an event, a singularity understood by those present to levy an obligation upon them waiting to be fulfilled throughout an indefinite future. The reception of the text by those present, and their subsequent acting upon the request with which it concludes, indicates as well that we can readily suppose their willingness to accept its use by Jesus,

47. Jeremias, *Eucharistic Words*, 169.
48. Ibid., 249–55.

Word and Deed

even severely modified, as fully legitimate and binding upon them, in spite of what they may well have regarded as its enigmatic character. It is both those modifications and the willingness of their hearers to accept both him and it that makes the text of Passover ritual live anew as a repetition in the singularity that was the anaphora of the Last Supper. But whether the singularity of that event plausibly qualifies any later fulfillment of the request by those to whom it was made or, by extension, by their followers or followers of later ages, as singular events is not at all clear, and it is that issue we must now consider.

. . . . of Many More

In objective terms it is impossible to ignore that there are very real differences between the Last Supper described in the New Testament and the liturgy of the Eucharist in Christian churches. The Eucharist as celebrated is not a Passover meal, is presided over by someone other than Jesus, is not held in Jerusalem, and is attended by persons who though nominally followers of Jesus do so primarily as members of a religion he did not know and who are at best only marginally thankful for the deliverance of ancient Israel. Differences like these, commonly glossed over through figurative means, speak eloquently against essentially naïve views of the Eucharistic liturgy that treat it either as a historical or as a spiritual reenactment of the New Testament Last Supper event. At one level we can consider this the fulfillment of Kierkegaard's skepticism over whether "it is possible to base an eternal happiness upon historical knowledge."[49] More systematically, it is critical to recognize that reenactments or restagings are bound ineluctably by the logic of events to become in Badiou's terms "normal," "natural," or "ordinary," i.e., no longer per se capable of singularity.

The logical core of this problem is, of course, the text itself, which in its repeated form loses the singularity of the original utterance. Further, that there is an established text to repeat raises once again the difficulty posed by Plato in the *Phaedrus*, namely that the written word relieves us of the obligation to remember.[50] Can we, in fact, "remember" the request of Jesus and respond to it adequately simply by repeating the text of the anaphora? If not a reenactment, what is the "remembrance" that fulfilling the request requires? And should it happen that a given liturgical event is

49. Kierkegaard, *Postscript*, 18.
50. *Phaedrus* 257b.

in itself some way unique or singular, what then is its relationship to the original Last Supper?

The most radical attempt to date to critique the Eucharistic liturgy as an event is that of Siobhán Garrigan in *Beyond Ritual: Sacramental Theology after Habermas*. Taking instances of clerical and congregational behavior observed in a succession of actual Eucharistic liturgies as Habermas's "conditions of possible understanding" provides her with the means to identify the social dynamic embodied in a particular liturgical event and, by extension, more generally characteristic of the persons and the group involved. The analyses that this technique produces are nothing if not frank in their exposure of conflicts and ambiguities that all too often lie unspoken, to the point of being rigidly unspeakable, in both congregational life and clerical behavior. Not all of the liturgies she reports on, however, are cast in traditional forms where lay/clerical dynamics would be the most obvious point of critical entry. Her observations on particular house-church liturgies of women's and gay men's ad hoc communities are especially valuable for illuminating how essentially separatist individual and group social identities, dedicated to inclusive social justice, subtly restructure the positions of celebrant and participants. True to the tenets of continental social theory, she considers liturgical action an arena for the practical expression of power, in the form of authority, by both individuals and the congregational group. In more socially traditional situations this presents itself primarily as a lay/clerical dialectic. In the nontraditional situations she considers, power is realized in a collective social identity wherein membership is the defining factor and the group itself is leader.[51]

Intrinsic to Garrigan's position is a recognition that liturgy does not happen as repeat readings of a ritual script, but as ontologically distinct occurrences, each with its own, using the Badiou terms introduced earlier, presuppositions and situation. Rituals may be performed according to established text and directions, but any effect these latter may have in their realization will be in large measure conditioned by those presuppositions. Her descriptions of different liturgical occasions clearly also evince a corrective intention to identity the sources of congregational conflict and pastoral difficulty with a purpose to resolving them. The overall result of those observations, however, is less a scale of degrees of social conflict or harmony, than a range of liturgical situations from rote performances with strong adherence to ritual procedure but marked by conflict to nontraditional

---

51. Garrigan, *Beyond Ritual*, 122–37.

liturgies in which conflicts are either resolved or effectively muted but the shape of the ritual has become to some degree ambiguous and unfamiliar. While it is indeed difficult to see the former as sacramental occasions, it can be difficult as well to recognize what the latter are sacramental occasions *of*. Further, as Garrigan admits, using liturgical behavior as an index of the congregational mind is not without its pitfalls, in that congregations are complex entities whose conjoint attitudes are often in flux, constantly moving targets for the outside observer who cannot, by definition, be completely privy to *all* their doings.

Garrigan's analysis focuses on the social dynamics of liturgical situations, bringing light to bear upon what are, often in emotional terms, their most poignant presuppositions. If we narrow our focus, however, from broad indices of congregational behavior to performance of the Eucharistic anaphora itself, additional conditions for understanding appear that are more epistemic in nature. Her insistence that the sacramental realization of any given liturgical action is shaped and conditioned by its presuppositions, particularly socially-oriented conditions of possible understanding, makes it clear that there can be no generic or all-inclusive descriptions of such actions, only reports based on direct observation. Simply attempting a generic description reveals the extent of difference that renders any celebration of the Eucharist individually distinct from any other. Some possible differences will, of course, seem—not without reason—trivial, until we recall that the pragmatic relationship of presupposition to situation is one where even otherwise insignificant conditions can be turning points.

Imagine, for instance, a liturgical situation set with all the customary appurtenances in a purpose-built church building, where the words of the anaphora, including the request for remembrance, are to be uttered as part of the service by a person authorized to do so by the congregation of those present. The congregation, including some visitors, responds appropriately at points indicated for them to do so in a printed program or service book. Hymns have been chosen prior to the service and are sung. Readings from the common lectionary scheduled for the day are duly read. A sermon or homily is offered by the celebrant. Ambient circumstances like weather and cultural or political events may be mentioned. The words of the anaphora, their order of pronouncement, their place in a liturgical sequence have been authorized by a larger ecclesiastical body operating within its own established textual tradition. Once those words have been said, communion of both bread and wine is offered by intinction to all those present.

Beyond the Body

Although such a description hardly exhausts the possible factors defining a liturgical situation, we can at least agree that it covers many of the most basic ones. In virtually all of them there is more than ample scope for differences that would separate this situation from any other. Some of these are broadly institutional, from qualifications for membership in the congregation, the manner of ordination, the regulation of the text, the order of the service, the choice of the readings, to the practice of communion. Others are more individually discriminating, as the personality of the celebrant/homilist, the distribution of the congregation within the liturgical space, the attitude in responses of both congregation and celebrant, and the hymns and music chosen for the day. Out of the control of all concerned are the unique and unrepeatable conditions of the day, from weather to current events.

Collectively these constitute a definite description of this service that distinguishes it from all others, not only those contemporaneous with it but all others in principle. The question remains, however, whether this justifies our thinking of it as an event, a situation fraught with consequences as was the original Last Supper, or even, in Kierkegaard's specialized term, a repetition of it. The question is what sorts of consequences we may be looking for, whether social or personally spiritual, and what may be their primary motivator. Feelings of greater harmony, social adjustment, or acceptance may indeed by occasioned by a Eucharistic liturgy, not by the act of remembrance itself, but only by the setting in which it was performed. Likewise, feelings of uplift and spiritual transformation experienced in connection with a service are far more likely attributable to a panoply of factors from musical setting and vestments to the homily or sermon; there is no particular reason to think of these as the effects of the anaphora. In short, there is no way, through the ordinary presuppositions of the liturgical service, to ascribe to it the same status as an event that we may ascribe to the original Last Supper. The effects and consequences that would make it so are rather those of particular presuppositions of the situation: setting, visual realization, comfortable companionship, acceptance, or thought-provoking speech. There is nothing to take as effects of the Eucharist that are not simply extraneous to it and, therefore, we must accept that at least on these grounds ritually-oriented liturgies very much risk mistaking the wrapping for the gift. Less ritually concerned groups of the sorts Garrigan describes can weaken their connection to the original Last Supper event because of their greater latitude in dealing with its text, but the dynamics of their group identities, socially interventionary in character, are in effect new tellings of the story of the followers of Jesus at the Supper, genuinely making them *repetitions* of it as Kierkegaard understood that term.

Perhaps the most pressing question that finally now needs to be addressed is what relationship exists, or should exist, between the text of the Eucharistic anaphora as uttered in the liturgy and the words of the original Last Supper. Is there a way in which the words used in the liturgy can rise above the serial redundancy of ritual so that the text functions in the tradition not simply as record or marker but as having at least the possibility of the event status that the original Supper has? Any answer to this must preserve both the role of the text as purveyor or vehicle of the tradition, as discussed earlier, and the value of liturgy as practically realized, even if not perfectly so. It would not after all do, exercising a Solomon-like rigor, simply to declare some Eucharistic services utterly meaningless ritual with no possible effect, more like trial runs of scenes in rehearsals for a play than religious acts. That one person's meaningfulness is another's meaninglessness is all too true, as is the inaccuracy with which we all too often decide what others are thinking.

As discussed at some length above, the request that is the performative center of the Last Supper anaphora constitutes, because of the obligation to respond that it puts in place, an event of far-reaching effect. The concept of event common in the philosophical tradition that atomizes occurrences, sandwiching them between past and future as the immediate results of discernible causes, leaves nearly altogether unspoken what either the logic or the status of any long-term effects might be. Alain Badiou's logic of events, on the other hand, lodges them in a historical milieu and, individually, in life-worlds that have an ontological status of their own. That such a view is not simply a romantic historicism is attested to by its clear analogy with the notion of the "light cone" in physics, that spatio-temporal area in which all the potential effects of an original event are located, what we might also call its "event shadow." Looked at this way, every liturgical use of the Eucharistic words, regardless of what might seem its rote or mindlessly redundant character, falls within the shadow of the original event and, however minimally or inadequately, acknowledges the terms of the request. This is not to say that there could be some uses that do not do so, ones wherein either the form of the words or the elements used are so altered from the original as to raise the question of their validity. But where challenges like these are lacking, that individual Eucharistic liturgies bear this sort of relation to the Last Supper gives them at least a very basic *ex opere operato* validity.

We also need to consider whether in some way the event status of the original Last Supper is somehow "shared with" or "participated in" by later uses of the Eucharistic anaphora. Although "share" and "participate" are terms very difficult to assign an intelligible meaning to in this case, there is indeed a way within the logic of events to draw a relationship between the original anaphora and its liturgical uses. While traditional event logic has difficulties accommodating composite events like the French Revolution, for example, in political or economic philosophies a great variety of occurrences can in fact stand as the presuppositions of a larger composite. All was not completed in the French Revolution, for instance, with the storming of the Bastille, but a great deal more went into its attempted transformation of French society, the effects of which are still very much evident in that country's law and culture. The logic of the Eucharistic anaphora, owing to the placement of the request for remembrance within the very narrative the enactment of which is its fulfillment, renders it in itself a presupposition of a larger, later situation that is comprised of the couple of the request and any given response to it. The event shadow of the request includes actual, as well as potential, couples, but only those intended as responses to the original request to "do this," that is, those undertaken in fidelity to the request rather than owing to any sense of ecclesial, social, or other religious obligation to ritual action. Every such faithful response, directed as it is to the original request, recognizes the extent of time between request and fulfillment, the historical life-world that is that event's shadow, both in that response and the obligation of other response to come. The person who communes faithfully in response therefore also communes with the "discernment" that Paul enjoined upon the Corinthians, a virtue of "fidelity" rather than of moral probity. It is a communion of the body and blood of Christ in that it is a response to those words as he used them, but it is even more a communion with the person whose words those *were* and, owing to the nature of the larger responsive event in these words are used, *still are*.

Lastly, does a performative understanding of the relationship between the original Eucharistic anaphora and its reuse in the liturgy contribute anything to solving the problem first raised by Kierkegaard about repetition? Can liturgical usage achieve, not through striking dramatic performance but by means of structured intention, the status as an event that the original Last Supper has in Christianity? In terms of its reuse of the traditional ritual of the Passover supper, the Last Supper in fact constituted a repetition of that ritual in retaining its textual presuppositions while still using them to create an entirely new eventual situation. Similarly, when a liturgical reuse of the anaphora occurs in a later time as a direct response to the request to "do this" it does indeed include those material details that comprise the circumstances of that particular performance, although these cannot of themselves define that situation as anything but a redundant, ritualizing reuse. Again, the response to the request to "do this" is a reply to the person of Jesus who made that request, a composite event irrespective of temporal and cultural difference that ever renews, repeats, the original anaphora.

5

BEYOND THE BODY

> ...nothing that ever happened should be regarded as lost for history. To be sure, only a redeemed mankind receives the fullness of its past—which is to say, only for a redeemed mankind has its past become citable in all its moments.
>
> —Walter Benjamin[1]

    Any characterization of Eucharistic belief that aims to avoid the pitfalls of traditional doctrinal approaches will need to prove it meets the needs of religious life and holds the potential to contribute significantly to its further development. The requirements for the success of that characterization are by and large the same as those that shaped the traditional approaches, keeping in mind, however, that there may be other, very different, ways to construe those requirements that point to critical aspects of Eucharistic belief traditional systematics were not able, for structural reasons, to recognize.

    The most salient feature of Eucharistic faith in both the Roman and the Reformed traditions is concern with an object, whether that object is what the words of institution literally say it is, the body of Jesus, or a benchmark for other religious concerns, including membership in the community, the action of grace, or remembrance of the saving work of Christ. Each generally, though there are certainly historical exceptions and anomalies to be accounted for, seeks further understanding through either

---

1. "Theses on the Philosophy of History," in Benjamin, *Illuminations*, 256.

Beyond the Body

the sorts of rational argument exemplified in late medieval scholasticism or the hermeneutic exploration of Scripture as a superior source of truth pioneered by the Reformation. To "step aside" from the Eucharist as object, to go "beyond the body," as it were, is also to step aside from each of these types of faith and their corresponding theological systems as well. In order to do so effectively we need to be clear about why each cannot fulfill its promise of an intellectual explanation that furthers faith's perpetual quest for understanding.

Two Types of Faith

We categorize Eucharistic beliefs as "realist" which, echoing the Council of Trent's usage of the terms *vere*, *realiter*, and *substantialiter*, insist on a local presence of Christ related to the bread and wine, the manner of that presence further characterized by terms of place like "in," "with," and "under." Every such use implicitly recognizes, even if only by exception, an ontology rooted in notions of substance that confers certifiably "real" status based primarily on physical existence. This link to physical materiality is reinforced by the not uncommon assumption that for an object to have an intelligible, "essential" identity it must be of a readily perceptible size.[2] Insuperable difficulties for a realist view emerge, however, as Beregarius of Tours famously noted to his misfortune, when we ask, primarily with the grammar of the sentence in mind, to what the "this" in "this is my body" may refer.[3] "In" cannot, after all, be simply equated with "inserted into" or "located in one part of," "with" cannot mean merely "next to," and "under" cannot refer to an independent substratum or underlayment, since there is only one, demonstrably singular, referent of the pronoun. And because that object is a physical one, the same laws of identity and difference that ordinarily apply to physical objects must apply to it as well. If we accept, as in commonsense we must, that no thing can be and not be the same thing, in the same way, at the same time,[4] "this is" is at worst a mistake and at best an equivocation. Those same laws of identity and difference further dictate that there can be no temporizing by degrees on the existential implications of that statement, since "this is" and "this is not" are utterly mutually exclusive.

2. *ST* 3a.77.4. Cf. Lindberg, *Beginnings*, 279 on *minima* and *minima naturalia*.
3. Macy, *Theologies of the Eucharist*, 35–43.
4. Aristotle, *Metaphysics* 1005b–1006a.

Beyond the Body

An uncompromisingly realist view of the sacrament courts the comforting assurances of its being "really" what it is said to be, but at the double expense of not knowing to what "this" might genuinely refer and of a logically necessary intolerance for all other views whatsoever. In terms of personal piety it localizes divinity as an inanimate object, so much so that, as unfortunately for Aquinas, the *personal* presence of Jesus as God in the Eucharist is only accidentally (by "concomitance") occasioned by the body and blood being there.[5]

If we limit controversy about the Eucharist to its identity as an object after the liturgical words of consecration have been spoken, any attempt to arrive at a broadly acceptable doctrine of it appears doomed. Even though it is indeed possible to agree that doctrinal contradictions could mask a mystery that all somehow can believe in, this is still a blind alley for further discussion and leaves unspoken the implication that claiming the privileges of mystery may be no more than an evasion regarding basic unintelligibility. Considering the centrality of the Eucharist in the Western tradition and that so much of the technical discussion of it has focused precisely on its identity as an object, it is scarcely surprising that the major Christian groups remain so far apart on this as on so many other issues.

Views we might, on the other hand, call "figurative," "symbolic," or even "allegorical" interestingly admit *prima facie* of characterization by degree, either by reason of the fragility of figures as symbols in the history of cultural change or by varying degrees of understanding in those who use them or are affected by them. The force of symbols like Trinity, Sin, Sacrament, Church, and even "God" has varied considerably over time as these may be more or less "fresh," "vivid," or "relevant" to many of the faithful in a given period. Where these are used in an official capacity in the liturgical and sacramental life of the Church, there is also question whether those who employ a figure or symbol without understanding it can in fact accomplish what was intended. Figurative language used in ignorance fails communicatively no less severely than ordinary, literal language can when it has strayed from lexical meaning.

There is an important distinction to observe between the notion of figure as applied to language and of figure as applied to objects. A word may be "used" figuratively or "metaphorically" in a phrase for the purpose of implying qualities in things, persons, and events that would otherwise escape notice should talking about them be limited to the narrow confines

---

5. *ST* 3a.76.1.

of literal description. Ignatius of Antioch's characterization of the Eucharist as "the medicine of immortality . . . the sovereign remedy by which we escape death," for instance, employs the terms "medicine" and "remedy" metaphorically for the effectiveness he believes the Eucharist has for personal salvation.[6] The history of Christian mysticism in the West is replete with similar usages, from the familiar "bread of life" (Jn 6:48) to the "bread of angels" of later piety. It is a test of the metaphoric character of such uses that we would not expect them to refer appropriately to percentages of one's body that had become immortal through reception of the sacrament or to fulfilling the dietary requirements of immaterial beings. But recognizing the limitations of verbal metaphor should not blind us to the logic of its power, which allows, within limits set only by propriety, that we may turn to virtually anything in our experience, real or imaginary, to broaden the import of what we refer to. It is a commonplace in the Western tradition of scriptural interpretation from Philo Judaeus through Augustine, Gregory the Great, and many more that of the two senses, figurative and literal, it is the figurative that points most dependably to the highest truth.

And taking the words "this is my body" figuratively or metaphorically has a long history. For Clement of Alexandria in the second century, for instance:

> Faith is more substantial, in fact, than hearing and is assimilated into the very soul and is, therefore, likened to solid food. The Lord presents the same foods elsewhere as symbols of another sort, when He says in the Gospel according to John: 'Do you eat My flesh and drink My blood.' Here He uses food and drink as a striking figure for faith and for the promise.[7]

Centuries later Ratramnus of Corbie would quote Augustine to similar effect:

> 'Except you shall eat,' says the Savior, 'the flesh of the Son of Man, and shall drink his blood, you shall not have life in you.' This seems to order a shameful crime. Therefore it is a figure, enjoining that we should have a share in the Lord's suffering, and that we should faithfully remember that for us his flesh was crucified and wounded.[8]

---

6. *Ignatius to the Ephesians* 20 in Staniforth and Louth, *Apostolic Fathers*, 66.
7. Clement of Alexandria, *Christ the Educator*, 37.
8. Ratramnus of Corbie, "Christ's Body and Blood," 127.

Beyond the Body

Still later Calvin, drawing upon both the late medieval genius for logical disputation and the Renaissance/Reformation passion for grammar and style:

> I say that this expression is a metonymy, a figure of speech commonly used in Scripture when mysteries are under discussion. For you could not otherwise understand such expressions as "circumcision is a covenant" (Gen. 17:13), "the lamb is the passover" (Ex. 12:11), . . . and, finally, "the rock from which water flowed in the desert "(Ex. 17:6), "was Christ" (1 Cor. 10:4).[9]

It should be noted in this last example that Calvin's higher truth is not a mystical or "anagogical" reality alluded to or hinted to by the words but simply the highest truth there is for Calvin himself, "the common usage of Scripture." For him a figurative interpretation is the only one possible, both as a faithful usage of Scripture and because a literal interpretation leads to superstitious rites and outright idolatry.[10]

When the larger literary context of "this is my body" within the Last Supper discourse in the synoptic gospels is taken into account, a second front relating to figure opens, namely, allegory and its cousin the "type." Here the discourse as a whole possesses an identity greater than itself, courtesy of a body of text or tradition to which it is considered to belong. One familiar example of a type or figure of the Eucharistic meal for the Patristic Age is the sacrifice of bread and wine by Melchisedech in Genesis 14, the two being related to each other as type or prefigurement and antitype or realization. There is also the question whether the ceremony of the Last Supper was itself somehow intended to prefigure in allegorical form the "sacrifice" of the Cross, and upon this projected relationship the Roman Catholic understanding of the Mass as a sacrifice depends in no small measure. Twentieth-century interpretations of the Eucharistic celebration in terms of liturgical history have also suggested that the Last Supper ceremony may itself have been deliberately cast as a typological reformulation of earlier ceremonies in Judaism.[11]

Finally, objects may themselves serve as symbols or figures. One of the earliest instances of this appears in the *Didache*, where the bread itself becomes a symbol of unity in the church: "As this broken bread, once

---

9. Calvin, *Institutes* IV.17.21.
10. Ibid., IV.17.35-37.
11. As suggested persuasively by Max Thurian in *Eucharistic Memorial*, passim.

dispersed over the hills, was brought together and became one loaf, so may thy Church be brought together from the ends of the earth into thy kingdom."[12]

Figurative language frees its user from the restrictions of epistemic realism and thereby opens broad vistas of evocative comparison between the mundane "this-ness" of something and the nearly limitless supporting context of all other reality. But it does so under two constraints. The first is that figurative usage depends heavily upon cultural context and custom for its effectiveness, thereby denying it any pretence of lasting certainty unless guaranteed by a higher authority, e.g., Revelation. Metaphors, figures, and symbols of necessity wax and wane in effectiveness depending solely on cultural circumstances. The second constraint is that figurative language about the Eucharist is unavoidably reductionist, a safe haven to fly to when ontological claims seem too demanding or occasion other sorts of difficulty. Calvin's "metonymy" depicts the Eucharistic words of Jesus as revealed speech acting true to form, but it speaks not at all to what the two poles of the metonymy might be. Where realist views of the Eucharist fail owing to their dependence on notions of physical place, figurative views leave unsatisfied the realist instinct for "this is" to be a reliable ontological reference.

Two Types of Theology

Similarly to the distinctions raised between realist and figurative approaches to the Eucharist, extended exercises in theological thinking have historically taken two different general forms. The first is the theological rationalism that extends in Western thought from Origen, through scholasticism in all its historical reincarnations, including the Lutheran Orthodoxy of the eighteenth century, to the existentialist theologies of the twentieth. The second, unfortunately not always seen as distinguished from the first, has a history that began in the New Testament itself and arguably reached its full stature in the biblicism of the Reformation. Based on the received meanings of texts as they are estimated to bear upon the principal theological issues of the tradition, this second form of theological thinking seeks mutual implications between texts and issues to use in constructing a satisfactorily complete description of the latter. Drawing heavily upon acquaintance with

---

12. *The Didache*, in Staniforth and Louth, *Apostolic Fathers*, 194–95. The same sentiment was echoed many centuries later by Ratramnus of Corbie, "Christ's Body and Blood," 138–39.

and memory of the texts, it operates primarily as an association of ideas as this is commonly understood. Each of these two modes of theological thought, which we can call respectively the "rationalist" and the "associative," whether separately or as often in practice intermingled, exemplifies the critical, analytic, and constructive qualities that have won them the label "systematic." The question we will need to address is whether either of these can helpfully illuminate the "this" in "This is my body."

Theological rationalism or rational systematics, sometimes characterized as "logical-linear" thinking, begins by establishing an initial stipulatedly rational basis upon which successive questions can be considered or assertions explicated in the light of common sense, logical argument, tradition, and divine revelation in Sacred Scripture. Its primary purpose is to arrive at a "scientific knowledge" through the method of "demonstration," the conditions for which are:

> (1) it must be something certain and not merely an opinion; (2) it will be a necessary, not a purely contingent truth; (3) it will not be immediately evident but known by reason of other evident and necessary truths; (4) it is derived from these latter truths by way of some form of syllogistic inference or discursive reasoning process.[13]

Aquinas's *Summa Theologiae* epitomizes this genre, demonstrating a structural minimalism and brevity of expression achieved by few other works of the period including, perhaps, others of his own. The *Summa* begins with the assertion of God's existence as an object, however different and unknowable, as foundation for and prelude to reflections on the nature of God, the Creation, the process of salvation and, much, much later, on means of salvation like the Eucharist. The macroeconomy of the work, its architectonic, is a linear progression through a range of issues embedded in a Neoplatonic narrative that begins with God and concludes in the return of all things to God. This narrative has roots in Christian experience as far back as the Gnosticism of the second century, the mystical works of the Pseudo-Dionysius, and Augustine's *Confessions*,[14] and it provides the work with both a progressive direction and a sequential agenda.

This narrative agenda, however, defines the *Summa* less as a work than does the microeconomy of its internal style. Successively posing the doctrinal issues implicit in the narrative as unresolved questions to be settled by

---

13. Wolter, *John Duns Scotus*, xvi–xvii.
14. Chenu, *Understanding*, 310–18.

argument and counterargument among reason, authority, and commonsense, imbues the text with intellectual risk, drama, and motion. Matters critical for personal life and the world as a whole are effectively subjunctivized, to be rescued not by reason alone or by Scriptural authority alone, but by dialectically reducing the allowance for doubt to as near the point of extinction as possible. An issue deliberately put in doubt must be intellectually sanitized as a condition for its becoming part of the foundational discourse of the larger narrative or, echoing the words of the New Testament, the stone that the builders rejected must become the cornerstone (Mk 12:10). The effectiveness of this technique for reducing doubt to certainty, introduced in the previous century by Peter Abelard, was guaranteed at least in part by the Augustinian conviction that evil being only the privation of good, doubt had only to be removed for certainty to be obvious.

A rationalizing analysis necessarily recommends that both the object and our experience of it are imbued with a noetic structure of universalizable, categorical character. The construction of a matrix of logically derived statements related to the object and the experience situates these as nodes in a structure of broad conceptual extent and intellectual authority. And when the very notions of reason and logic are additionally taken to be manifestations of an infinite divine reason or *logos*, the rationalist religious thinker readily sees that to understand one truth is have at least an inkling of all the truths there are or ever could be, including even the concept of truth itself. Perhaps the most striking aspect of such an intuition is that it implicitly imputes ontological status to reason and reasoning, relying upon a sense that these, and the truths they reveal, can somehow be said to "exist." In response to the practical objection that it would be impossible for any individual to know all the truths that are or could be, the theological rationalist resorts to a personal eschatology in which all truths will be available in a single glance through the direct knowledge of God, the heavenly reward of the blessed.

As powerful as theological rationalism may be, it cannot escape what are essentially its fideist roots: to accept one of the articles of faith is to accept all of them, due allowance being made for the effects of ignorance, perversity, or misunderstanding on the process. Such acceptance is made possible, however, only by the prior acceptance of reason as authoritative, an acceptance that is in the end rooted in culture and personal history rather than logic. And while the web of syntactic reasoning exercises a powerful attraction on anyone in search of either intellectual or religious certainty, its charms cannot in the end produce any statements with the ontological certainty required for thinking of something, in fact of *anything*, as a "this." The existential limits of reasoning are nowhere more apparent than in proofs for the existence of God, which can demonstrate the reasonableness of there being a divine existent without ever being able to reveal that existent itself. Regardless of the cogency of argument, in the end it is cultural values that are decisive: "And this all men call God."[15]

Exemplified in works as diverse as Calvin's *Institutes*, the *Loci Communes* of Philip Melancthon, and the *Loci Theologici* of, respectively, the Lutheran Martin Chemnitz and the Roman Catholic Melchior Cano, "associative" systematics emerged in the Reformation as a counter to the metaphysical know-nothingism of late medieval nominalism. Although these works all differ somewhat in their overall plans, they share an agenda of subjects dictated by catechetical and sectarian apologetic concerns. For Calvin the articles of the Apostles' Creed supplied the agenda, while Melancthon first culled his list of subjects from the succession of the prophetic and apostolic books (the *Loci Communes* of 1535), but turned later to the Apostles,' Nicene, and Athanasian creeds for this purpose (preface of 1555).[16]

Shaping larger works of theology according to a catechetical agenda was not in itself a Reformation innovation. Aquinas had, after all, ambitioned much the same thing in the *Summa Contra Gentiles*. What distinguished these later efforts was an internal microeconomy that conscientiously rejected the mechanism of the question and its resulting resolution through dialectic on the grounds that the central propositions of the faith ought never to be placed in doubt, no matter how constructively intended:

> Even if philosophy teaches that there must be doubt about those things which are not perceptible to the senses and are not principles and are not corroborated by demonstration, ... yet we know that the doctrine given to the church by God is certain and immovable even if it is not subject to the senses, is not innate in us, as principles are, and is not discovered by demonstrations. But the cause of this certainty is the revelation of God, who is truthful.

---

15. *ST* 1ae,2.3.

16. For Melancthon's list see Manschreck, *Melancthon*, xlix–li. For Chemnitz, see Preus, *Loci Theologici*, 41–43. For Melchior Cano, see Curtius, *European Literature*, 552–53.

Therefore we should never permit this philosophic doubt in regard to the teaching which has been given by God to His church.[17]

In place of the ladderlike progression of resolved difficulties, the *loci* or topics format begins by borrowing from classical rhetoric, particularly as found in Cicero's *Topics* and the pseudo-Ciceronian *Rhetorica ad Herennium*, the notion of a conviction or concern shared by all as part of common experience or, putatively, as common sense. In the forensic arguments that had been Cicero's concern, an appeal to one's natural, commonsense desire to preserve his or her own life, for instance, provides a compelling justification for having wounded someone mistaken in the dark for an attacker. Medieval rhetoric, lacking the social *mise en scène* of the Roman law court, had treated topics rather as popular literary devices employed to bring about particular effects, as in an author seeking sympathy from readers at the outset of a work by lamenting his insufficiency for the task.[18] Regardless of such a difference in setting, however, the medieval use of standard tropes still constituted an appeal to a common experience, that of the literary tradition, as its criterion.

Despite the reliance that Melancthon placed, particularly in his earlier work, on the *loci* as common, shared perceptions and experiences of a sort that no one could doubt and that could readily serve as *sedes argumenti* or wellsprings of argument,[19] it is hard to escape the feeling that for the *loci* to be cast this philosophically is still somewhat at odds with his basic priorities. Faith for Melancthon, as for Luther and for Calvin as well, cannot simply be a matter of following the most obvious human instincts of thought. The reality of sin alone renders that impossible. Melanchthon expressed this perhaps best in the Preface to the 1535 edition of the *Loci*:

> For the teaching of the church is not derived or drawn from demonstrations, but from those statements which God has given the human race in sure and clear testimony through which in His great kindness He has revealed Himself and His will.[20]

---

17. "Preface of Philipp Melancthon to His Theological Topics," in Preus, *Loci Theologici*, 35.

18. Curtius, *European Literature*, 83–85

19. See Schneider, *Melanchthon's Construal*, 73–78.

20. "Preface of Philipp Melanchthon to His Theological Topics," in Preus, *Loci Theologici*, 35.

Beyond the Body

From their origins as reliable, nearly trite sources of argument, the *loci* thus became those "places" in Scripture that are the only true sources of doctrine. And the linear dialectic that had structured high-medieval scholastic theological thought came to be replaced by a hermeneutical reason primarily intended to promote consistency among the conclusions to be drawn when multiple loci are associated with each other. Given that the God of Scripture cannot lie, this turns the problem-posing and problem-solving program of the medieval *Sic et Non* into, quite simply, one of *sic* alone, where constant, confident affirmation rather than questioning is the rule. The resulting model for systematic theology thus comes to resemble something long familiar to structural anthropologists, who have pictured religious cultures as contained sets of decision-making points.[21] Subgroups within the culture, Protestants and Catholics in an overall European Christian culture for example, have issues like grace, church, and Scripture in common but make very different decisions about each of these. Some issues, like the doctrine of the Trinity on the other hand, have nearly always been objects of general consensus after an initial period of strenuous debate. Despite such differences, however, the overall character of theological argument in the *loci* model is that it begins from authority, particularly scriptural authority, rather than from rationally accessible first principles.

The most common criticism of associative theological thinking is that it devalues reason and argument in favor of a textual authority that cannot credibly be ascribed to any set of human documents, however venerable. But this does little more than rehearse the Enlightenment's Age-of-Reason difficulties with both the text of the Bible and the historical reliability of biblical "witness." Worse still, it simply pits the cultural values of one age, the Enlightenment, against those of another, the Reformation. That associative thinkers pay little heed to such well-worn criticism should be no surprise. A more serious, and more contemporary, issue than the probity of the biblical text, however, is the problem we investigated earlier in chapter three, the simple fact that it is, after all, text, i.e., writing. Quite aside from the endless problems posed by language, manuscript traditions, and cultural differences among the ages, the biblical written resources are finite objects whose number and content have been fixed and limited by common agreement, by human custom. In contrast to the potentially infinite extent of thought available to the theological rationalist, the associative

---

21. See, for example, Leach, "Genesis as Myth," 1–13. An even closer analysis of binary structure in myth appears in Lévi-Strauss, "Four Winnebago Myths," 15–26.

thinker must always remain captive within the constraints of the available text. The response that the text, despite its limitations, is what God has deemed necessary and sufficient for our salvation, begs the question of just how comprehensive in content a text would have to be for it to speak fully to the vast panoply of human experience and to the even greater extent of human intellectual ambition. Most telling, however, is that the best, and perhaps the only, device within the associative mode of thinking for dealing with something referred to as "this" is to establish relationships among texts that will supply it with something approaching a definition. But this also is bound to be an empty hope, given that textual relationships must always take the form of typologies, metaphors, allegories or, recalling Calvin's term, metonymies. Definition by metaphor may be illuminating in terms of emotional and memorative association but inevitably leads attention away from the object of reference to those that have been posed in comparison. To know what *those* are is simply not to know what "this" is. In the end, neither the ontological intuitions of rationalist thinking nor the associative linking of thoughts or forms of words can suffice to reveal the object to which "this" refers.

The Task of an Antitheology

The inability to arrive at adequate object definitions renders it impossible on formal grounds for either of these two traditional forms of theology to provide satisfactory accounts of the Eucharist when considered a physical object, no matter how unusual a one. To go on then to declare that the person of Christ is experienced in the Eucharist as a matter of "natural concomitance" by relating it to his resurrection, continuing life, and divine unlimitedness merely deepens the dilemma for the believer by adding layers of revealed assertions equally outside the normal range of intelligibility. Among the first steps, therefore, for anything aspiring to be an antitheology is to repudiate two assumptions: 1) that physicality is the standard for existence and 2) that revelation is transcendently true. If we wished to give a name to the sort of position this suggests, we might well choose the one characterized by Alain Badiou as "dialectical idealism."[22] In (very) broad

---

22. Badiou, *Theory of the Subject*, 116–24. It is possible to detect some Platonizing ambiguities in Badiou's avowed materialism. The discussion of the multiple and the Void that plays such a foundational part at the outset of *Being and Event*, for instance, seems to leave untouched the peripheral intellectual perception, that had certainly troubled

outline, this treats the existence of material objects as matters perhaps of fact but not of interest except for their inclusion in events that both constitute and alter the "world" of the knowing subject. In contrast to the world of objects that comprise the Aristotelian universe and are acted upon and changed by causes, the world of "coming to be and passing away,"[23] dialectical idealism's "world" is comprised largely of events, including those that involve texts like those of revelation, that are the collective past of experience and the presuppositions of its ongoing composition and character.

Modeling an antitheology on the antiphilosophy that Badiou attributes to Wittgenstein suggests a further set of requirements. The first is that it must take the stance of a critique of what we can broadly characterize as "traditional" theological language. "Critique" refers here not to the Sisyphean cultural task of interpretation in its many forms, but to an ongoing intention to raise foundational questions of the sort that provoke crisis about the value of that language as it is both used and understood. Such a critique must risk as well venturing into the Pyrrhic circularities of the debate about truth, must lodge its certainties in world and moment, forsaking aspirations to a more empyrean home. The second is to take into account the social forces at work in the theological tradition, forces hidden within the texture of intellectual and religious working life that foster excessive formalism, whether Aristotelian, nominalist, Kantian, existentialist, or any other. Further, it must take its place in the world as an activity rather than as a text to be treasured for its content.[24] As in our earlier discussion of text, repetition, and moment in Kierkegaard, text is only truly realized when its reading is a moment of difference that steps beyond redundancy as an event that is quite new. Revelation is not a sous-text lurking beneath its own

---

the early Wittgenstein, that 0 is not simply the absence of 1, written as ~1, standing for "not–1": "The fact that in a certain sense the logical form of p must be present even if p is not the case, shews symbolically through the fact that "p" occurs in "~p." Wittgenstein, *Notebooks*, 21e. See also Badiou, *Being and Event*, Meditation Four, "The Void: proper name of being," 52–59.

23. Perhaps Aristotle's clearest statement of this is in *De generatione et corruptione*, on acting and being affected and on actuality and potentiality. Aristotle, *De generatione* I.8.326b,29–I.9.327a,29.

24. Badiou, *Wittgenstein's Antiphilosophy*, 75–82. It would be possible, of course, to build a theological system based entirely on Badiou's thought, an enterprise for which his carefully developed and defined terminology would be particularly useful. For an intimation of how both intensive and extensive a possibility this offers, see the remarkably perspicuous assessment of Badiou's thought presented by Hollis Phelps in *Alain Badiou*, 121–68, "Badiou's Theology."

words, awaiting deliverance into meaning, but a higher-order text revealed only in the event constituted by that moment. Lastly, it must believably lay claim to be sufficiently different to represent a genuine innovation.

There are, of course, caveats to be observed about this. One is that an antitheology cannot be simply the negation of theology, particularly if we take the easy road to defining theology minimally in saying only that it is "talk about God." On the one hand this would lead to the recharacterization of religious language as concerned with something less intellectually stressful than the concept of God, ethics for instance. On the other it could lead to an anti-theological, and anti-ecclesiastical, pietism of the sort that flourished in Germany in the seventeenth and eighteenth centuries. Another is that while an antitheology's remit certainly entitles it to be critical of established theology, this still does not license it to dismiss theology wholesale, owing ironically to the fact that it too is no less context bound by its own presuppositions. Further, an antitheology also bears the same responsibility to prove its own case in an intellectually respectable and communicative manner, to argue coherently and convincingly rather than merely ranting. Lastly, an antitheology needs to prove that it can operate credibly within the ambience of its own surroundings, the seeming wasteland of postmodern thought comprised of what remains to us of the Enlightenment after decades of serial deconstruction.

Alternate Criteria

Where traditional forms of faith and their corresponding theological types are committed of necessity to the development of true propositions about the Eucharist as an object, the logically pragmatic nature of the performative "do this" in the Words of Institution suggests an entirely different range of criteria for a satisfactorily intelligible faith. The first of these is that the event that transpires through liturgical action be somehow "real," not in the sense of the physically dimensive "real estate" that the Council of Trent's *realiter* evokes to distinguish a physical existence of the body of Christ from that of possible, notional, or "intellectual" property, but as a disruptive, transformative, interventionary event involving actual persons, living or dead. The second is that this event happens completely in the present moment rather than through introspection or recollection, i.e., it is not an imaginative projection into a remembered past, nor is it essentially defined by any other characterization than what it is, a request or command. Lastly,

Beyond the Body

it is an event that affects those involved in it on a completely personal basis, changing them through its occurrence. It should not be overlooked that while these three criteria of real, immediate, and personal are related first of all to performative language use, they also correspond closely to the concepts of event, world, and subject developed in an entirely different context by Alain Badiou.[25]

Real

The most critical aspect of the Eucharist in the life of faith is a contact with the person of Jesus, one that is neither imaginary nor illusory. What we might call "substantialist" understandings of such an objective presence seem suitably real until we realize that "substance" is a metaphysical rather than a physical category of understanding. More problematically, it provides only a noetic guarantee that where the substance is, a personal presence will also be. A purely symbolic understanding of that presence will likewise not do, in that it deprives it of any but emotional or associative significance. And, finally, claiming a "ghostly" or "spiritual" presence, as those terms are typically understood, would be even less satisfying, in that a paraphysical presence could only limit or lessen the experience, rendering it more naively miraculous than mysterious, more a matter of superstition than of orthodox belief.

Adumbrations on the subject of being "real," particularly in regard to religion, often show an unfortunate tendency to take "real" as a representative term for all those "values" that a particular culture holds most dear, regardless of whether it overtly articulates them. For such an essentially idealist understanding of the human thought process, those values function as "ideals," in comparison with which the objects of experience are judged both to exist and to be of a certain nature defined by them. The relationship between culture and "reality" is thus a causal one in the most classic sense, culture determining that something is, what it is, how it is, and what its place is in the overall scheme of things. The phrase "culturally determined" eloquently represents the near-universal reach of culture as an explanatory concept. That explanatory force dims, however, when we consider not only how resistant to complete description any particular culture is, or how tenuous the necessity may be for any free individual member of it

---

25. Badiou, *Being and Event*, 201–11, 391–409, 506–7, 522–23; Badiou, *Logics of Worlds*, 598.

Beyond the Body

to act according to its "norms." The same, unfortunately, is also true of more sophisticated idealizing characterizations of the real as the proper object of *a priori* categories of experience, where hope of an explanation appears through analysis of religious situations in which something "wholly other" or "mysterious and fascinating" is experienced.[26] A closer look, again, reveals that in such experiences mundane physical objects serve merely as triggers for feelings of awe, fear, or exaltation that, although more powerful, are no different in kind from their ordinary manifestations.

At the opposite pole from cultural determinations of the real is the situation of the single experiencing individual, for whom the real is very much "in the eye of the beholder." By simple analogy, what is real must be at least as real as the beholder's own experience in that event and have, as it were, *locus* or place within it, keeping in mind that not everything involved in an event need be a physical object. This last qualification speaks directly to the structure of complex events as temporal phenomena. Illusion, hallucination, and self-deception stand not as criteria for validity, but honor in the breach the implicit universalizability of that experience.

Immediate

The "presence" of an object is not, of course, a quality or attribute of the object itself, but designates rather that it is an element of an event, that event being the experience of someone *to* whom it is present. On a prima facie basis this means simply that the experience is not (nor could it be) of something historically past, just as it cannot be of an object or event yet to come, recognizing déjà vu and second sight as exceptions to the rule rather than contradictions of it. That which is present is directly before us, immediate in the sense of being most proximate to us in this very moment. Both past and future can be "distant," suggesting a span of time sufficient to separate events in each of them quite definitively from the present. We also refer to events as in the "immediate past" or the "immediate future," referring thereby to their serial proximity to the present, a proximity that may allow of their being included in a more temporally relaxed or expansive designation of the present, as in the "present" or perhaps "current" decade, in contrast to the last or next century. A presence occurs in the immediate present, in a bounded unit or period of time referred to more narrowly as an "instant" or, slightly more expansively, as a "moment."

26. Otto, *Idea of the Holy*, 25–30.

Beyond the Body

Corresponding to this temporal sense of immediate there is also a relational sense of being direct or unmediated. That something is immediately clear to me indicates not only that it so now, in the present moment, but also that there are no intermediary steps of understanding involved, as there would be if it had become clear "accidentally" courtesy of some unrelated factor. Similarly, an immediate presence would be a distinguishably individual one in its own right, rather than one realized through another object or event acting as symbol or stand-in. Thus the presence of Christ in the Eucharist is not identical to the presence of the worshipping community, or even to the visible bread itself. Images ranging from gathered grains of wheat to the mystical body of Christ amplify the experience of presence by building what is in effect a lifeworld around it, but they expose us to the danger of living in the periphery of what is present, rather than directly within it. Again, characterizing the Eucharist as a sacrifice, or even as a thanksgiving, is to step away from the domain of immediate, confrontational presence and into the realm of religious or theological discourse.

Personal

The requirement that a Eucharistic presence be personal is defined by two factors. One is our direct experience that a body without life is not a person but simply the body of a person who once was. The other is that perennial skepticism, learned from life, about the reliability of physical evidence as a real indicator of human character. The optimistic basis of such skepticism is the hope for something durable and constant about an individual that we can rely upon. The theological tradition bears witness to several different ways of understanding the person, beginning with the Latin *persona* as a translational equivalent of the Greek *prosopon*, the individual we meet. The need to situate Christology intelligibly within the context of Trinitarian doctrine in its turn occasioned a further characterization of the person as agent or actor, formalized in the term *hypostasis*. In various parts of the tradition this latter term also came sometimes, confusingly, to be equated with both *ousia* or being, and *physis* or nature.[27] Two of these concepts, action and identity, figure significantly in performative speech acts. A

---

27. *Westminster Dictionary of Christian Theology*, s.v. "Person," by R. A. Norris and "Hypostasis," by Frances Young. For a more recent discussion, see Marmion and Van Nieuwenhove, *Introduction*, 72–73.

performative speech act, after all, *does* something, and the identity of the speaker in that act is critical to its successful performance.

The first problem we face, however, is that the primary paradigm for identity in a personal presence is not other minds objectively external to ourselves, but the mind as present to itself. This, despite its seeming Cartesian certainty, represents a limiting condition, in that, in the words of Augustine, we can only know others insofar as we can know ourselves.[28] Personal self-presence can range in intensity of focus from thinking by internally vocalizing one's thoughts (talking to oneself) to direct, unthinking, contemplative awareness. Its greatest advantage is that no demonstrable effects of such a presence are required or expected. Its greatest disadvantage is its limiting idiosyncrasy: a personal presence in the Eucharist that is myself writ large simply will not do. Even though I am indeed the person who is there to me when I am in a room alone, it will still take memory (and history) to establish a legal or forensic persona corresponding to that self-awareness. The absence of demonstrable effects of another's presence in the Eucharist forestalls from the outset the possibility of a constant, durable personal identity established along such psychologically oriented forensic lines. It does not, however, remove from our consideration the social and logical presuppositions governing the distinctive identities of the persons who are speaker and hearer in performative speech acts. The speaker simply is that person who is speaking, identified first and foremost as the agent of that speech act. Forensic considerations may indeed bear upon whether the speaker is someone entitled to perform that act, but the necessity to establish this arises completely from demands regarding the legitimacy ("happiness") of the act itself and is durable for only so long as the act has relevance to anyone.

Founding a concept of identity on the self-awareness of the subject raises the further question, hinted at earlier, whether we are treating that virtually "transcendental" self as if it were a durable physical object. While this course of action may be useful for modeling some intuitions we have of the notion of presence, it would be misleading for us to take it as foundational. As Derrida pointed out in his early critique of Husserl, assuming the existence of a transcendental subject underlying thoughts and actions like speech events represents a step away from an empirical method, even

---

28. "For whence does a mind know another mind, if it does not know itself?" (Augustine, *On the Trinity* 9.3).

a phenomenological one, and a step toward a metaphysics.[29] While we may have freed ourselves from thinking of the Eucharist as a physical object through conscientious "bracketing," for the identity of a "real" presence to be tantamount to the existence of a durably objective, knowing self reintroduces the same problem in a more subtle, but still more problematical, way. Again, all we need to know or can know in a performative speech act is that the speaker simply is the person who is identifiably the agent of it.

These difficulties ease somewhat when we recognize that persons as we experience them are neither physical nor metaphysical entities but the *loci* and originators of actions directed to us. As the real is to some extent in "the eye of the beholder," the person is the one who is acting. doing something that affects us. An action is "personally" meant when it has been directed "personally" by one single individual to affect one other single individual, namely, me. The most basic logical identity of this person is as the speaker, the agent, an identity that can be delegitimized but never taken away.

The Problem of "Presence"

The philosophical and theological traditions of the Christian West have struggled over the millennia either to reconcile or to separate the reality of being from that of acting. Over the course of that history each of these categories has also itself been divided. Being (τό ον) has included both that which we can sensibly perceive and that which we cannot, such as ideas, universals, or other abstractions of a higher order (τα νοητα). Acting likewise divides readily into visible events and occurrences or the potential for bringing those about alluded to under the headings of power or potential (δύναμις). It is clear that our description of the Eucharist in the previous chapter is of an event comprised of an original action, a request, that set the stage for further actions in response intended to fulfill its terms. Focus on this as a performative speech act enables us to emphasize the direct relationship between those who participate in the Eucharistic liturgy and the person of the historical Jesus. It also enables us to define such participation in terms of response, rather than either attendance per se or worship understood as reverencing, honoring, or acknowledging a superior being or deity, the most lexically representative characterization of religious worship in general. Most importantly, what is done in response is the repetition,

29. Derrida, *Speech*, 5–7.

understood as Kierkegaard meant that term, of a collective event uniquely transformative in character and thereby of ongoing influence in the worlds of those participating.

While we can certainly say that the person of Jesus is that of a conversation partner to whom a believer responds directly in the Eucharist, it is notably less obvious that this thereby constitutes a "presence" as this is ordinarily understood. For a postmodern period when the notion of "substance" has largely yielded to the physical ambiguities described by quantum theory, and the supposedly necessary connection between persons we know and their physical selves may become strained or even dissolved by reason of neurological conditions, arguing for psychic presence on the basis of physical presence can no longer rely upon a forensic commonplace like "natural concomitance."

Further, there are difficulties involved in the very notion of "presence" itself that need to be addressed. The first of these derives from the traditional identification of presence with existence, i.e., that to be present means to exist in the "here and now."[30] If, however, as Kant first noted, existence is not a predicate, one must ask whether this applies to the concept of presence as well. Ordinary usage, owing perhaps in English to medieval philosophical precedents, tends to treat both as substantives capable of being qualitatively modified, as in an "imposing" presence or a "bleak" existence. Closer examination of each of these cases, however, reveals that they refer to any of a series of judgments by an external observer in particular instances over a period of time that amount to what we now call samplings. There are perfectly good reasons to suspect that in the interstices between those samplings that person may have experienced visible instances of devastating self-doubt or enjoyed happier moments than those which had been observed. To be present is to be recognized as being able to be counted or characterized by an observer at a particular moment and in a particular place. While we may "count on" that object or person being present on some later occasion, this is not in principle reliably so. "Present" is only and always present *to*, and this may likewise be extended to the notion of existence. In distinction from classical idealism, however, we need not deny the existence of objects when they are not in our view, but rather hold simply that they do not matter to us in such moments.

---

30. A theme investigated with great depth and perceptiveness by Hans Urs von Balthasar, for whom this suggests that the only philosophy capable of dealing with this question is an existentialist one (*Presence and Thought*, 19–23).

Beyond the Body

Ordinary usage suggests in this as well that presence is not only a state that can be qualitatively described but a form of activity. Although nothing more than bearing, facial expression, and dress—"the state of her appearance"—may be involved, an imposing presence "imposes." And, once again, we can collect successive instances of noticing this that imply it is an activity that takes place on occasion over time, maintaining likewise the reservation that there may be moments when we ourselves or others might see things differently. But presence is neither an activity, especially an ongoing one, nor is it any state other than that which allows that which is present to be counted as such.[31] "Presenting" oneself does not make one any more present than was already the case by reason of being there. References to "presence" in the Eucharist that imply a state, characterized as "real," or an activity of being there fall well short on formal terms of telling us anything more than this.

Despite such difficulties, it is undeniable that belief in a presence of Christ in the Eucharist holds a prominent position in the tradition of Western religiousness. Although much of Protestantism in the Reformation rejected it, particularly in regard to reservation of the Sacrament outside the context of the Mass as a practice redolent of superstition and idolatry, reverence for it nonetheless remained strong, particularly among Lutherans and later among Methodists. As the ecumenical movement of the twentieth century moderated some of the differences among Protestant groups and theirs with Roman Catholicism, the liturgical movement refocused interest on the Eucharist as the central worship activity. Too commonly, however, such interest was directed more to technical possibilities for resolving the "realist" and "symbolist" differences described in outline above than to assessing the prospects for a personal piety or spirituality of the Eucharist.[32] That such a need both exists and calls urgently for attention has thankfully also become more generally recognized.[33]

---

31. The verb to "present," on the other hand, with reference to supplying one's credentials, introducing an acquaintance, or transferring possession of an object refers indeed to an action, a performative speech action.

32. Most notable in this regard is the proposal that the Eastern Orthodox concept of "transelementation" serve as a *via media* for reconciling Reformed and Roman differences over the term "transubstantiation." The problem with such an approach is that it necessarily limits itself to formulating the concept of presence in terms of change, whether physical or metaphysical, in the Eucharistic elements as objects, leaving little room for thought regarding whose presence that might be and how that might affect those present other than as worshippers. Hunsinger, *Eucharist and Ecumenism*, 315–16.

33. For United Methodists, for instance, this had been an issue for some time:

Beyond the Body

From the Council of Trent in the sixteenth century into the modern period, the expression "real presence" has referred to the body and blood of the historical Jesus *being there*, as it were, in a particular place, although just how particular was very much a matter for discussion.[34] Eucharistic hymns in the Latin liturgy were more concerned with adoration than with prayer. Similarly, the art-historical phenomenon of the "Gregory Mass," portraying an appearance of the sacrificial Passion over the action on the altar, points the viewer to the process of salvation overall rather than to the intimate concerns of personal redemption. If we think of "real presence," however, as referring to a person, it is not until the nineteenth century that such a concept seems to become possible, reflecting more than anything perhaps both the very intellectual individuality of the Age of Reason and the introspective emotionalism of Romanticism. The founding story of this new notion appears in the life and preaching of the Curé d'Ars, the Roman Catholic St. John Vianney (1786–1859), who one day asked a simple peasant who spent hours in church simply staring at the tabernacle that housed the reserved Eucharist to explain what he was doing. His reply, "I look at Him, and He looks at me," became a standard in Catholic piety ever after.[35] Deceptively simple, it accepts the doctrine of existence in place but regards it as no more than an anchor for a personal relationship that is a continuing action of uninterrupted mutual response:

> The man who communicates loses himself in God like a drop of water in the ocean: it's impossible to separate them anymore. If you only thought of it, in these vast deeps of love, there's enough to lose yourself for all eternity.[36]

"... the laity 'feel a deep need for Eucharistic spirituality based upon fuller understanding and more meaningful practice'" (Gayle Felton quoted in Saliers, "'Taste and See,'" 229).

34. As in, for instance, the discussion in *ST* 3a.76.5 and 6, regarding whether the body of Christ in the sacrament is present both locally and in such a way as to be moved.

35. "Un paysan, passant du temps tous les jours devant le tabernacle, disait: 'Je l'avise et il m'avise . . . ' Si vous passez devant une église, entrez pour saluer Notre Seigneur. Pourrait-on passer devant la porte d'un ami sans lui dire bonjour?" (Quoted on the website of the Missionnaires de la Très Sainte Eucharistie, a lay/clerical group dedicated to perpetual adoration of the Eucharist. http://www.adoperp.com/adoration/saints/curears.html). This story also appears in the text of the current edition of the *Catechism of the Catholic Church* under the heading of contemplative prayer: [2715] "Contemplation is a gaze of faith, fixed on Jesus. 'I look at him and he looks at me': this is what a certain peasant of Ars used to say to his holy cure about his prayer before the tabernacle" (http://www.vatican.va/archive/ENG0015/__P9M.HTM).

36. Trochu, *Curé d'Ars*, 103.

Beyond the Body

And the nature of that relationship, however modestly described, is an intellectual one, reflecting the perennial association of visual with mental perception. Egalitarian at heart, it situates both perceivers in a polar union where matching mutual regard is all that is required. If additionally we recall the adage that the eye is "the window of the soul," it presupposes that this is a regard between living persons who are actually there, rather than merely their bodies.

Increasing personalism in Eucharistic piety is also detectable in a lexical shift that occurred with regard to the word "communion," particularly as "Holy Communion." In the wake of the Reformation, the concept of communion was primarily a social one, denoting an assemblage of individuals who together, as authorized members, joined in celebrating the Lord's Supper, a feast held, as it were, "in common" by a "community." Receiving the Eucharist, communing, in such a context served to witness the status of participants as belonging to an eschatological assembly of the saved, the "communion of saints." There are as it happens, however, other senses of commune and communion, most notably those referring to an active intentionality toward an object or situation with which there is thought to be some mutuality of awareness.[37] Poets of the Romantic age communed with nature or with their own souls, not to mention with the souls of other like-minded persons as well. Prayer, where it occurred, would most likely take the form of dialog between discrete individuals. Although still part of a rite of passage to more advanced membership in the Church, Holy Communion, particularly for the first time, became one of the milestones of the spiritual life. The *Story of a Soul*, the autobiography of St. Thérèse of Lisieux (1873–1897) tells of her first, and subsequent, communions in just such terms. One can find perhaps no more telling description of the intimacy of this experience than hers:

> Ah! how sweet was that first kiss of Jesus! It was a kiss of *love*; I *felt* that *I was loved*, and I said: 'I love You, and I give myself to you forever!' There were no demands made, no struggles, no sacrifices; for a long time now Jesus and poor little Thérèse *looked at* and understood each other. That day, it was no longer simply a look, it was a fusion; they were no longer two, Thérèse had vanished as a drop of water is lost in the ocean. Jesus alone remained.[38]

---

37. *Oxford English Dictionary* (1971), s.v. "commune," "communion."
38. Thérèse of Lisieux, *Story of a Soul*, 77.

Instances like these illustrate the importance that personalism as the sense of mutual contact or even dialog has in the most vibrant Eucharistic piety. Each, however, depends disconcertingly much upon the assumed presence of a second person who is actually (i.e., physically) *there*. We can, of course, ask whether the "look" of the peasant and the saint is only metaphorically meant, for both the worshipper and the worshipped. But if so, the question then painfully arises whether this is really only an accident of the physical imagination not unlike our efforts at remembering the exact place where something was that we have lost or mentally picturing someone at the table with us who we wish were there but who in fact cannot be. Cases like these, lying as they do on a continuum of examples that includes both hallucinations and children's invisible friends, leave us justifiably wondering how much we should rely on them as exemplars of faith.

Curiously, religious experiences of presence like these were contemporaneously of interest not only to those most actively involved in lives of piety, but to those of a philosophical or psychological bent as well, for whom the study of beliefs and practices had become an occupational calling. In *The Varieties of Religious Experience* under the heading of "The Reality of the Unseen," William James described several cases of persons who had experienced powerful but invisible presences.[39] Although in only one of these, and that but momentarily, was overt physicality ascribed to whatever was present, all attested "feelings" of presence that were just as powerful and convincing as those associated with perceptible physical objects. More importantly, in every case those who had these experiences felt them to have been events of great significance in their lives. In one very poignant instance a person who had once depended upon them over an extended period for emotional support found that the loss of them left his life somehow bereft of meaning.[40] James also provides one example related to the reception of communion:

> Sometimes as I go to church, I sit down, join in the service, and before I go out I feel as if God was with me, right side of me, singing and reading the Psalms with me.... And then again I feel as if I could sit beside him, and put my arms around him, kiss him, etc. When I am taking Holy Communion at the altar, I try to get with him and generally feel his presence.[41]

39. James, *Varieties*, 61–71.
40. Ibid., 66.
41. Ibid., 71.

Beyond the Body

These cases proved something of a problem for James, who clearly would have preferred to find simple, empirical explanations for them. Their lack of visual content, not to mention the obvious respectability of the subjects themselves, makes them unlikely candidates for classification as hallucinatory. The suggestion that these feelings of presence have been triggered by "association" with other ideas or experiences he dismisses easily on the grounds of the complete disanalogy of their objects with those of any genuine perceptions. He also declines to explore that Kantian avenue of opportunity, not long after investigated by Rudolf Otto in *The Idea of the Holy*, of an innate sense or Kantian "category" by which we are able to perceive a unique class of objects broadly characterized as "holy."[42] As seems generally the case throughout the *Varieties*, James remains content to suggest that the occurrences of these experiences are verifiable, even if the existence of their objects is not.

We might, of course, stop here, as James does, respecting the claims of those who experience ghostly other-somethings, comforting spiritual presences in their lives, or the person of Christ in the Eucharist while refusing to speculate further on either their veracity or their validity. The motivation to do so is based first on the rather empty empirical standard that reports of experiences really do refer to experiences, and second on the rather mild conviction that there may be, after all, more things and of different kinds in the world than we are intellectually capable of comprehending at the current stage of human development. It presumes as well that the most important feature of such experiences is that they are of some *thing*, some object, much like the "ectoplasmic" objects that had fascinated Victorian devotees of spiritualism.

But perceptual experiences like these are, by definition, *of* something, events in which a perceiver is acted upon by a stimulus, whether external or internal, a stimulus to which the perceiver then directs attention. The mental state corresponding to this attention, philosophically referred to as "intentionality," is one in which the perceiver may look at, listen to, explore tactilely, taste, sample, and so on. So long as we use physical perception as a paradigm for intentionality we are safe both in affirming that such experiences have occurred and in maintaining our reservations about the existence of their objects.

When the intentionality of a mental act is broadened to include cases of thinking, specifically thinking *of* something, matters complicate. I can

---

42. Ibid., 61–62; Otto, *Idea of the Holy*, 112–16, 136–42.

think of or direct my thoughts to, not only things that are impossibly far away spatially but which may not exist physically at all. I can think about the concept of equality, the number four, or Gödel's theorem, whether as names or in more intimate detail as intellectual or logical puzzles. Likewise, I can think about a comforting presence or something lurking in the room outside my field of vision, all valid instances of intentional awareness regardless of their physical status. What I cannot think of, however, except by name, is objects or concepts that are implicitly contradictory, e.g., square circles and the like. We might, if we wish, say simply that in such cases there is no "there" there to think of, but only the effort of intentionality itself. Thinking of the Eucharist as the physical body and blood of Christ, while prima facie unlike thinking about a square circle, nonetheless requires us to use referring terms like bread, flesh, wine, and blood in ways that can only be validly descriptive in situations that are either miraculous or deceptively manipulated in the manner of cinematic special effects. We can say that such usage is logically contradictory in that when we say something is a kind of thing that it cannot be, except in a metaphorical, analogical, or figurative way, we have said it is something that it is not. Saying that we see the Eucharist *as* the body of Christ gets us no further, for the same reasons. Most damning of all, while the very logic of intentionality links the perceiver to the perceived or the thinker to thought, it does not at all necessarily allow us to extend the perception or the thought to other objects, however closely related.[43] Thus, while we may gaze as intently and lovingly as we wish at a consecrated host, this in no logically acceptable way entitles us to infer the presence of a psychically endowed person with whom we can converse or who we become through the act of taking communion. Bringing to mind once again the criteria suggested earlier for descriptions of Eucharist belief, there is no denying that experiences like these of presence are both strongly personal and vividly immediate. Therein, however, lies their problem, in that however personal they may be, there is no way to characterize them that allows for a communicable validity outside the experience of one person. They may be very real for that one, but are not necessarily so for any others, even those who believe themselves to have had cognate or similar experiences. Though undeniably personal and direct, they fail to have that dimension of public communicability that the use of "real" requires.

43. Making use here of John Searle's distinction between "intentionality-with-a-t and intensionality-with-an-s" that limits how extensively we can derive other valid assertions from statements referring to an intentional event, whether it be of an object perceived or merely thought about (Searle, *Mind*, 174–78). See also Searle, *Intentionality*, 24, 180–96.

Beyond the Body

There is, of course, a second kind of intentionality that we must consider here, namely, that exemplified in the thinking-of that we see in language use, as this affects not only the logical possibility or impossibility of a presence of Christ in the Eucharist but our ability to think about the Last Supper itself, in which the command or request to "do this" occurred, as an event. As mentioned earlier, we can speak referringly about a great many things that though not actually present to us here, we can talk or think about without being exposed to challenges of absurdity. We can do this without any intellectual problems whatever about the other side of the moon even though it is highly unlikely we will ever have the opportunity to inspect it ourselves at first hand. Having heard enough times that the moon, like the earth, is round, we include statements to that effect in the repertoire of accepted premises upon which other, inferential, statements can be made, e.g., that there are probably craters there as well, and so on. But while the visual circularity of the moon as it appears is undeniable, further inferences about its shape depend largely on information that comes to us from language alone, language that conveys either the conjectures or the experiences of others. In the normal course of events, it would be impracticable, solipsistic in fact, to dismiss language about objects that others have perceived but we have not on the grounds that only perceptually-based intentionality will do. Cultural artifacts like maps and travel descriptions, for instance, would on that account amount to no more than social blather. The structures of both society and language speak to and support the utility in terms of survival of accepting the knowledge of others about the world. Despite the necessity of this in practical terms, however, there must remain the lingering proviso that such knowledge may be either incorrect or in some manner mistaken, skewed, or even deliberately deceptive. Accepting it represents an act of faith in those persons from whom we learned to talk about such things, and it is always subject to revision pending the arrival of further information. In short, can we accept or agree with claims for a presence of the person of Jesus in the Eucharist or about the event that it is based upon simply because others have taught us to speak of it? The answer is, of course, yes, so long as that answer remains a completely provisional one, leaving untouched whether faith in that event or that presence is at all more than simply faith in those others, that is, in this case, faith in the Church.

But the logic of intentionality as it plays out in language is more complex than our discussion so far has allowed for. Language provides us with names employed by others to refer to and describe things, and using these we can direct our attention toward particular objects, being able even to think quite plausibly about them in the absence of direct perception. In principle, although not necessarily in fact, we may indeed take the trouble to court direct acquaintance with them and thus add our personal perceptions to what we have learned through the social mechanics of language. What, however, are we to do when such corrective opportunities are not in principle available, particularly with regard not to persons or objects but to events. Although this might not be so difficult with regard to classes or types of events, especially as these may enjoy a history of calculated definition in legal or forensic terms, nothing more than a reversal of the "arrow of time" of theoretical physics would do for us to be able to augment our acquaintance with past events. One important facet of this problem is the ambiguity of language in quantifying over events, in that objects and persons "exist" or have existed, whereas events "occur" or have occurred. The sense of this distinction becomes more pointed when we consider that another sort of temporal entity, a "state of affairs," is often said to "exist," as well as, like events, somehow to effect change, reflect the priorities of those involved, alter history, and so on. The relationship between states of affairs and events is a curious one, in that the former can properly be said to contain the latter, which in its turn can bring about change in the overall state of affairs. Further, where states of affairs can readily be defined in terms of the four-dimensional coordinates familiar from twentieth-century physics, including participating persons or objects, determinate physical locations, and recorded chronological times, events may be comprised of entire sequences of such states of affairs. In book eleven of the *Confessions* Augustine despaired not only of his lack of ability properly to explain time but to definitely describe events as well, on the grounds, reminiscent of the motion paradoxes of Zeno of Elea, that neither future nor past actually exists, the present is at best elusive, and that, consequently, there is nothing fixed or fixable on which to pin a description. The extent and seriousness of the problem this presents is evident in that the event in question for Augustine was the creation of the world described in the first chapter of Genesis, epitomized in the single term "beginning," as in "In the beginning. . . . "

While Augustine's problem calls for a different solution, intentionality directed at a past event like the Last Supper, and specifically to the command or request to "do this," may not in fact be subject to the requirement that it be in principle anchored in or verified by the possibility of direct acquaintance. This is owing to the potential for certain kinds of events, specifically those like performatives, to serve as an element or constitutive part of one or more later composite events. Such a situation is made possible first by the interventionary character of the first event, namely to mark a difference from the state of affairs at the time it occurs and to achieve the completion of its conditions for fulfillment only in a subsequent event that occurs in direct response to it. The temporal separation of these two parts is of little consequence, given that together they comprise a single request or response occurrence anchored definitively in the present. The most important aspect of that anchoring, however, is not simply that it is present, but that the composite occurrence of request and response represents the product of an interventionary moment that thereby becomes constitutive of the "world" of the responder. Given that the dynamic content of the request, and of this very request in particular, was so in contrast to the Passover ceremony that was its traditional setting, it can also be readily envisaged that the world of the one making it would likewise per se be comprised of both that interventionary moment and the expectation of its potential responses. The world of Jesus at the Last Supper and the worlds of those who "do this" intersect at this juncture such that the personal identities of each are logically active in the event. There is, after all, no one else but the one making that request to whom the response is directed, regardless of either physical presence or absence. Insofar as these worlds are joined, the connection made is real in the sense of being experienced in the present, exclusively the experience of those two participants, and thereby completely personal.

The Presence of Christ and the Presence of God

But although we can establish that a liturgical response to "do this" is one pole of a composite event that is, as it were, independent of the normal restraints of time, that event still depends for its validity on an alleged "fact" of history, viz., the use of those words at an historical Last Supper. Further, although experienced in the present, a "doing-this" event still fails to provide the sense of simultaneity that colors most accounts of presence, both sacramental and otherwise. Historical reenactments are, after all, predicated on the assumption that the past is indeed no longer available. Once again Kierkegaard's question about the relation of faith to history arises: *"Is an historical point of departure possible for an eternal consciousness; how can such a point of departure have any other than historical interest; is it possible to base an eternal happiness upon historical knowledge?*"[44] We need not go to the lengths Kierkegaard did in suggesting absurdity as the philosophers' stone by which faith can transcend history,[45] but we do need to recognize that the contingency of our knowledge of the past renders the historical Jesus, despite the testimony of Paul and the Synoptics, much less than an object of absolute knowledge or absolute certainty. Although surely represented in the liturgical response to "do this," the historical person of Christ is inferentially available therein only on the basis of our trust that it is indeed he who was the past partner to the present action, a situation we might with some chagrin christen as presence by a merely "logical" concomitance. The success or failure of any attempt to tie liturgical action to the historical Jesus, therefore, depends intrinsically upon finding a solution to Kierkegaard's problem, which we can readily paraphrase in three questions: Do historical events "exist" in any way other than as "past"? Is there anything more substantial about historical events than that we can direct thinking intentionally to them? Lastly, what place can historical events have in the configuration of a human world of experience or lifeworld that is more than the continuation of the normal, the routine, the ordinary? Ancillary to all these, but critical for Eucharistic piety and devotion, is the further question whether there is or can be any sense of simultaneity or presence in our experience of those events.

In the phrase "the practice of the presence of God" the Western spiritual tradition bears witness to a broader use of the term "presence" than that described by either William James or the Curé d'Ars. God present as an implied or projected conversation partner has, of course, always been a feature of prayer, epitomized in the psalms and elaborated in the literary tradition that reaches from Augustine's *Confessions* to the *Imitation of Christ* and beyond. The ascetic practice of the presence of God, however, is distinct from prayer, being, in fact, intended both as a necessary preliminary to prayer and as a means to extending the intentionality characteristic of it to quotidian experience. Nicholas Herman, generally known under his religious name of Brother Lawrence of the Resurrection (1614–1691), advocated precisely such an approach:

> That in order to form a habit of conversing with GOD continually, and referring all that we do to Him; we must at first apply to Him

44. Kierkegaard, *Postscript*, 18.
45. Ibid., 345.

with some diligence: but that with a little care we should find His love inwardly excite us to it without any difficulty.[46]

The result of this practice over time is clear: "by often repeating these acts they become *habitual*, and the presence of GOD is rendered as it were *natural* to us."[47] The development of this habit enabled Lawrence to live, sometimes almost continuously, while directing his thoughts to God, so much so that "he was more united to GOD in his outward employments, than when he left them for devotion in retirement."[48] Although founded initially on an intellectual recognition of the "providence and power of GOD,"[49] this sense of presence is by no means an intellectual or noetic one: "we ought to make a great difference between the acts of the understanding and those of the will; that the first were of comparatively little value, and the others all."[50] The great power that this sense of presence had in Lawrences's emotional life suggests that it went well beyond conscious efforts toward God as an intentional object, to genuinely mystical experiences:

> And I make it my business only to persevere in His holy presence, wherein I keep myself by a simple attention, and a general fond regard to GOD, which I may call an actual presence of GOD; or, to speak better, an habitual, silent, and secret conversation of the soul with GOD; which often causes in me joys and raptures inwardly, and sometimes also outwardly, so great that I am forced to use means to moderate them, and prevent their appearance to others.[51]

Underlying such mystical perceptions, however, is the foundational belief in a providence that continually cares for him, the "high view of the Providence and Power of GOD, which has never since been effaced from his soul . . . and kindled such a love for God, that he could not tell whether it had increased in above forty years that he had lived since."[52]

Protestant interest in the practice of the presence of God found its most articulate advocate in Jeremy Taylor (1613–1667), whose *The Rule*

---

46. Lawrence, of the Resurrection, *Practice of the Presence of God* in *Brother Lawrence*, 10. Dozens of popular editions and translations are presently in print.
47. Ibid., 22.
48. Ibid., 14.
49. Ibid., 7.
50. Ibid., 22.
51. Ibid., 25.
52. Ibid., 7.

and Exercises of Holy Living, first published in 1650, remains one of the most frequently reprinted titles in Christian devotional literature.[53] Like Brother Lawrence, Taylor's concept of the divine finds its initial footing in nature but with an intimacy of example rich in both intellectual and emotional associations:

> God is wholly in every place, included in no place, not bound with cords (except those of love) not divided into parts, not changeable into several shapes, filling heaven and earth with his present power, and with his never absent nature. So S. *Augustine* expresses this article. So that we may imagine God to be as the Aire and the Sea, and we all enclosed in his circle, wrapt up in the lap of his infinite nature, or as infants in the wombs of their pregnant Mothers: and we can no more be removed from the presence of God than from our own being.[54]

Going on to describe further ways this may be so, Taylor begins with the divine essence which, owing to its infinity, cannot be limited by either the extent or the qualities of any given place. Reprising the distinction beloved of the scholastics between absolute and ordained divine power,[55] he further proposes that God is present by that power, manifested across a wide range of perceptible phenomena, a being who both "roules the Orbs of Heaven with his hand" and "hardens the joynts of Infants." Every creature, including some we might only be able to imagine, are included in the extent of his rule. God is present also in the world at large, in places specifically dedicated to worship, in the hearts of all through his Holy Spirit and, lastly, within each conscience.[56]

Although Taylor, like Brother Lawrence, is careful to include "*frequent colloquies* or short discoursings"[57] between God and the soul as a practical

---

53. There are currently over a dozen popular printings and editions available. Few if any of these, however, show much interest in Taylor's monumental depth of scholarship in both the classics and the history of Christian doctrine. A critical edition of *Holy Living and Holy Dying* edited by P. G. Stanwood has restored some of their original text. Material from other of Taylor's works cited here is from Heber, ed., *Whole Works* (1839). William James mentions Taylor as a recognized source of Protestant interest in the practice of the presence of God, James, *Varieties*, 103. Taylor enjoys popularity with Roman Catholic audiences as well.

54 Taylor, *Holy Living*, 35
55 For example, Duns Scotus, *Ordinatio* 1.44 in *Will and Morality*.
56 Taylor, *Holy Living*, 35–36.
57 Ibid., 39.

part of the exercises, it is plain that these are ancillary to the fundamental experience of presence that structures his world as a whole. Despite its homiletic character, Taylor's list of perceptions delineates, item by item, the elements that comprise a composite description of all that was for him, recalling again Wittgenstein's phrase, "what is the case," those situations that conjointly constitute a constellation of events in temporal place that are definitively his and his alone. There is nowhere, however either inspiring or off-putting, that is empty of God, nor anywhere that his guiding influence can be thought absent. The world we see reflects the glory of a God not standing somehow above or behind that glory but within it. God's presence for Taylor is not a presence *of* but a presence *to*, one equally structuring of experience whether it be in natural surroundings, social gatherings, religious assemblies, or normal human converse.

Most importantly for our purposes here, God for Taylor is also present to history, not the temporal continuum that history would be for the eighteenth and nineteenth centuries, but all those events, good and bad, that comprise the individual's world, or life, as known to God. Although not a little Calvinist in tone, Taylor's portrayal of God as "the *great Eye* of the World, always watching over our actions" nonetheless manages to avoid any hint of predestination, suggesting rather that a sense of the divine presence provides the most effective means for promoting moral uprightness. Among the "rules" he lists for the practice, he includes "an *habitual dread* and reverence towards God, . . . that Judge who is *infallible* in his sentence, *all knowing* in his information, *severe* in his anger, *powerful* in his providence, and *intolerable* in his wrath and indignation."[58] Yet as one of its benefits it also "produces a *confidence in God*, and fearlessenesse of our enemies, patience in trouble, and hope of remedie."[59] As its greatest benefit it provides that "we are always in the sight and presence of the Allseeing and Almighty God, who also is to us as a Father, and a Guardian, a Husband, and a Lord."[60]

Unlike Brother Lawrence, who was seemingly content to accept a realist doctrine of the presence of Christ in the Eucharist,[61] Taylor acquired

---

58. Ibid., 38–39.
59. Ibid., 41.
60. Ibid., 42.
61. Even while occupied with his work in the kitchen, he could "still possess God in as great tranquility as if I were upon my knees at the blessed sacrament" Lawrence, of the Resurrection, *Brother Lawrence*, 20.

considerable repute as an opponent of the Roman doctrine of transubstantiation. Quite aside from his historically based reasons for arguing against the necessity for that doctrine being promulgated at all, he insists that belief in the Eucharist is a matter of spiritual, rather than physical, knowledge. While on the one hand this is unsurprisingly similar to arguments that had appeared as early as those of Zwingli at the Marburg Colloquy, it is hard not to notice, as above, the same spiritual perception clearly operating in Taylor's understanding of those events that make up the structure of his world. In this regard his position stands as generally consistent with the nominalist tradition in pre-Reformation, late medieval thought, for which rational (or rationalizing) proofs for the existence of God were either unnecessary, impossible, or counterproductive for the devotional life.[62] Underlying this but wholly unacknowledged is the broadly spread distinction, much debated in medieval logic, between terms as used in either referring directly to particular qualities of individual objects or to those qualities as universal in meaning or application. Known technically as distinguishing between terms of "first" or "second" "intention,"[63] this proved particularly useful for explaining how one might refer accurately, relying upon the established conventions of language, to objects that were not present to perception.[64] Given that the meanings of universal terms could be learned only through experience and could refer only to things in principle available to sensory experience, a nominalist reading of terms of second intention precluded them from use in reasoning that would in any way lead to metaphysical conclusions.

Limiting reason to spoken and written language, however, left untouched less easily resolved questions about the activity of the intellect with regard to those things referred to by terms of both first and second intention. Under the heading, therefore, of *intentionality* as a state of mind, and ignoring or denying the total unknowability of abstract universal qualities or divinity itself that had earlier prompted the Thomistic doctrine of analogy, thinking intentionally, particularly in connection with second intention, came to be thought of as having a grammar and logic of its own. Duns

---

62. Taylor never refers to the existence of God as an issue for doubt or dispute. See "Index of the Principle Matters Contained in Bishop Taylor's Works," in *Whole Works*, 1:266.

63. For a cogent description of the canonical nominalist understanding of this distinction, see Buridan, *Summulae*, 968 n. 182. For Buridan's own use of it, see idem, 2.3.5, "The Description of the Individual," 118–21.

64. Pasnau, "Cognition," 288–90.

Beyond the Body

Scotus' (1266–1308) proposal of the univocity of being[65] made possible the grammar of thought later proposed by Pierre d'Ailly (1350–1425)[66] and the ultimately mystical hermeneutic of Nicholas of Cusa (1401–1464), who resolved the Thomistic problem by embracing a different way of knowing. Despite the confessional and ecclesiastical distances that separate them, Cusanus' declaration that "truth is the object of the intellect and can only be seen in an invisible way"[67] seems less removed than we might expect from Taylor's description of Eucharistic faith: "We hunger after him, not with a corporeal appetite, but a spiritual" and "for in true divinity, real and spiritual are equipollent."[68] The ancient distinction of language as spoken, written, or mental[69] sorts comfortably with Taylor's ability to hold conclusions about the nature of both God and the Eucharist that are suggested simply by the shape and tenor of his own world. He is well aware of the ninth-century debate over the differences between literal and figurative interpretation and recognizes that faith demands more than the latter can supply: "I suppose it to be a mistake, to think whatsoever is real must be natural; and it is no less so to think spiritual to be only figurative."[70]

Returning to the problem posed by Kierkegaard about the availability or usefulness of history for belief and salvation, Taylor's gratitude for the general benevolence of Providence, the benchmark for his manner of reasoning in general, leads him to situate the institution of the Eucharist as an event not merely in human history but in that of the cosmos overall:

> As the sun, among the stars, and man, among the sublunary creatures, is the most eminent and noble, the prince of the inferiors, and their measure, or their guide: so is this action, among all the instances of religion; it is the most perfect and consummate, it is an union of mysteries, . . . it actually performs all that could

---

65. "I say that God is conceived not only in a concept analogous to the concept of a creature, that is, one which is wholly other than that which is predicated of creatures, but even in some concept univocal to Himself and to a creature" (Duns Scotus, *Philosophical Writings*, 22).

66. For whom "mental propositions were thought to have a grammar like that of spoken or written propositions" (Kneale and Kneale, *Development*, 230).

67. Nicholas of Cusa, "Letter to Kaspar Ayndorffer," 272

68. Taylor, *Whole Works*, 1:163. For his complete treatment of the subject, see § ix of "On the Real Presence of Christ in the Holy Sacrament," idem, 9:503–12.

69. Kneale and Kneale, *Development*, 229.

70. Taylor, *Whole Works*, 3:293.

necessary for man, and it presents to man as great a thing as God could give: for it is impossible any thing should be greater than himself.[71]

Or, in eschatological terms, "as Christ is the Lamb slain from the beginning of the world, so shall he be the food of our souls in heaven . . . in this world to live the life of the Spirit, in the other world . . . to live the life of glory."[72]

Liturgy and Time

Problems of history like that of the reliability of the text in reporting the words of Jesus at the event of the Last Supper are basically problems about time. The foremost of these is the inaccessibility of prior events, owing to the directionality of the "arrow of time," the characteristic irreversibility of certain classes of events wherein a series of changes concludes by closing off any possibility of returning to the conditions prevailing at its start. When a glass is shattered, or its contents spilled, attempts to restore the original situation are capable of only incomplete or marginal success. As the author of Ecclesiastes noted, this is likewise true of life itself, once "the silver cord is snapped, and the golden bowl is broken."(Eccl 12:6)

The notion that at least some events of the past are retrievable or that their once-upon-a-time occurrence can be verified depends on one hand upon the social conventions of a culture for its plausibility. Historical information is communicated on lines dictated by custom and authority as those are configured in the given society. It depends as well, on the other hand, upon the reservoir of common experience for which, despite the constancy of change, some things can be depended upon, including even, curiously, the irreversibility of certain kinds of events. That an event occurring in the immediate present, i.e., *now*, will in a few minutes or a few hours be in the past certainly does not mean that it is not now occurring or that any persons or objects now involved in it do not exist. How this event will later be described or identified can, of course, raise some interesting questions. Was a remark a charitable one or a veiled insult? Did the words of institution define a ritual, make a request, or simply beg for prayers? Even empirical verifications depend upon the conditions stipulated in

---

71. Ibid., 3:289.
72. Ibid., 15:416.

advance for their fulfillment, leaving open ever after the question whether the substance of the judgment made was of the evidence per se or of only a prejudiced portion of it. Although the future's view of what is happening now will suffer the constraints of what is best described as a probabilistic hermeneutic, common sense demands that we not discount the existence of events simply on the grounds that we may later misunderstand them. In purely commonsense terms, occurrence in the present is the primary guarantor of references to that present in the future. The same is true, *pari passu*, for prior events as they may feature in present or future mentions.

That the present becomes past as it moves ahead into the future is the primary feature of what is known as *perceived* or continuous time, a benchmark distinction in current discussions of the subject.[73] Perceived time, even when it seems to flow slowly, still *flows*, moving relentlessly onward, as does the present itself. Events scattered across this continuum are characterized not as "present," "past," or "future" of themselves but related to each other simply as earlier or later. Perceived time is identical with temporal experience and cannot for practical purposes be separated from it, primarily because temporal experience is always and only in the present. Thinking about earlier events as past, as objects of intentional thought, may be directed to the past but occurs wholly and completely in the present. It is precisely because of this that perceived time has no implicit boundaries. We cannot mark a point for when the present begins, nor likewise for when it ends. In this sense the present is, as it were, time*less*, a characteristic that defines what we might call its temporal horizon. There is no limit other than a practical, informational one for how far into either the past or the future we can think intentionally, and everything we think of in this way occurs in present thought, i.e., simultaneously.

Although perceived time seems prima facie limited to events of which we have had direct awareness, the general dependability of the past for reference in the present suggests that events prior to or outside such awareness can feature in present temporal experience. Such events belong properly to that other domain of time we think of as history, time that is documented rather than perceived, that is measurable, divisible, countable, as well as datable and therefore "factual." Since our knowledge of these events depends upon documentation, this is sometimes referred to as time

---

73. This concept has come to play a part in contemporary discussions in physics on the nature and/or the reality of time. Barbour, *End of Time*, 19–20.

Beyond the Body

of record or recorded time.[74] Owing to its quantitative character, it is readily imagined as a quasi-spatial body, progress through which by motion is measured along another dimension as a parameter, rendering it a Newtonian absolute that is rather an analog of perceived time than its basis. The relationship between perceived time and that of recordable events is, in the proper sense of the term, a pragmatic one, in that perceived time is selective in its attention to the majority of the exceedingly many events that surround it in daily life. While the situation or placement of extra-experiential events in history depends upon the conventions of record, their placement, if any, in perceived time may not. The proper function of those events that somehow cross over the threshold from the many, the regular, and the ordinary, is an interventionary one in that they alter the configuration of the events that comprise the body of perceived time that is the "world" of the perceiver. How that alteration may occur is, again, pragmatic rather than logical, in that an intrusive and unwelcome but documented fact may or may not become part of that world. Insofar as that fact refers to an event that is directly contradictory of one or more of events in that world, it occasions a crisis that can be resolved either by incorporating the event into the perceived world as a whole or by dissolving that world altogether. As part of history, recorded or documented time, claims about events like these are verifiable or falsifiable either in practice or in principle. To feature in a world of perceived time, however, they need be verifiable only in principle, leaving room without penalty for provisional or even counterfactual beliefs. Room is also left thereby, however, for hermeneutics in that recorded events or collections of them may be seen in perceived time as related in ways that transcend facticity. Where previously unknown or unacknowledged occurrences can have an interventionary effect upon the makeup of a world of perceived time, the structure of that world can also intervene in determining what will be thought of as history.

Returning once again to Kierkegaard's question, an event that is part of recorded or historical time is limited to that time in both its importance and its effect. As part of a world of perceived time, however, it owns both an immediacy in thought and, thereby, a simultaneity with its original occurrence. Perceived time is, owing to its potential limitlessness, the time of Kierkegaard's "eternal consciousness," and it is in this time, rather than in

---

74. Ibid., 30–34. His distinction of perceived from record time is indebted to the historic paper by J. E. McTaggert, "The Unreality of Time."

that of record, that the event of the Last Supper, including the request for remembrance, is part of the believer's world.

One who comes to the Eucharistic liturgy comes in perceived time. This is not a matter of "attending" or "participating," but simply of responding to the original request to "do this" by being somewhere in order to do so. Although "attending" church amounts in lexical terms to no more than merely being present and accounted for, a suspicion lingers in the very use of the word that attending is something one *does* with discernible effect, like walking as in walking a well-marked trail. Either directly or indirectly, attending and participating both imply objects, in that one may attend and participate *in* a service as a scheduled, datable, historically recordable event. Attending and participating occur in recorded rather than perceived time, and so each is of itself falsifiable, in that one can be counted as present without being either attentive or involved in the same liturgical action as others who may be there. Paul's prophetic enthusiasts and self-indulgent Eucharistic banqueters in the first letter to the Corinthians (1 Cor 11) serve as a case in point.

The worshipper's "world" of perceived time includes on the one hand the complex of presuppositions that shape the action, the performance, of responding to the original request. Some of these may be, as it were, local, in that they are particular to the person responding, as in emotions or feelings of hope, anxiety, and the like. Underlying these, however, is the temporal structure of world discernible in the writings of both Brother Lawrence and Jeremy Taylor, a perception of benevolence, a feeling of gratitude for that benevolence, and an expectation of its permanence in the future. Although this perception may be expressed in theistic form, that is, divinity is attributed without question to this benevolence, its experiential or "first intentional" basis is the general friendliness that physical reality, the universe as a whole, has shown human life. Owing to the limitlessness of perceived time and to the concomitant limitlessness of what it may apply to, it is equally reasonable, in a commonsense way, for this to be a benevolence without bounds in either physical or temporal extent, i.e., an infinite one.[75] The relationship between the worshipper and this benevolence is not only one of gratitude, but of dependence as well, insofar as the expectation of it in the future is warranted by its having continued from the past into the

---

75. Reflecting here Wittgenstein's remark: "If we take eternity to mean not infinite temporal duration but timelessness, then eternal life belongs to those who live in the present. Our life has no end in just the way in which our visual field has no limits" (Wittgenstein, *Tractatus*, 147).

present. This pragmatic expectation serves as a paradigmatic justification for second-intention conclusions in general, but in particular for identifying events in human history as related to divine purpose. It is the logical basis for Taylor's spiritually, rather than materially, perceiving the body and blood of Christ in the Eucharist.

In the perceived time of the liturgy, both the text of the liturgical structure itself and of the readings determined by the lectionary repeat things that have been said and done before, but in an order and selection unique for the day. Where written texts may be read silently as visits, as it were, to their historical past, texts read aloud, as Catherine Pickstock observed, become altogether present in doxological use.[76] The relationship they bear to each other in their datable pasts, however, yields in present perception to their overall placement in the world of the worshipper, that is, not to whether one comes before or after the other historically but whether one or the other stands out to the worshipper on the grounds of its meaning.[77] Although both text and actions in the liturgy may already be well known, their occurrence in the liturgy is by both design and accidental circumstances unique, offering per se the opportunity for what could be a recurrence of the ordinary, the routine, the déjà vue but more appropriately a repetition in the Kierkegaardian sense in which actions or text reconfigure the constellation of events that comprise the world of the worshipper. The situational intent of the sermon or homily is either to bring the texts of the liturgy and readings to this point or to become such a point in its own right.

In the Eucharistic liturgy, all, regardless of status, calling, or ordination, are responders to the request to "do this." Viewed as occurring in historical time, the original text suggests a narrow, minimalist understanding in which it is the physical actions of Jesus that are to be mimetically reproduced in remembrance, not the overall event of the Supper itself and the request that is its focal point. It is this minimalist account that requires we believe something historically transformative occurred at the recitation of the words of institution. From the same point of view derives as well the centrality of the priestly role in the liturgy upon which notions of church hierarchy are based. But the request occurred not as history but as an interventionary step outside the history of both Passover and sacrifice in Israel,

76. Pickstock, *After Writing*, 220–52.

77. Introducing here the concept of an ordering of events in perceived time that is independent of distinctions either between past and present or earlier and later. McTaggert had identified such independent ordering as a "C-series" distinct from either perceived or recordable time ("The Unreality of Time," 461–64).

as the adamantine difficulty of the words of institution themselves amply demonstrate. The obligation it levies on the responder is the same as that upon those present in the original event, namely, to be there at an event deliberately done in its image. In such an event, one among those present says the words, but all respond in remembrance. It is the response of all that fulfills the conditions of the request, not the repetition of either the role or the words.

In historical time it matters that what the worshipper receives in communion is somehow the result of a change or transformation. This is true, as it happens, even if we take the part of Ratramnus, for whom a sacramental transformation through grace, like that of Baptism, was the model. In the timelessness of perceived time, however, there is no historical gulf to be bridged that requires change in a durable, physical object in order to guarantee lasting effect. What is critical rather is that the world of the worshipper come to include the event of the original request as an event that is as transformative now as it was for those who were present then. By answering the call to remembrance the worshipper hears the words as they were said and by the person who said them, regardless of the intervening centuries and regardless as well of the difficulties of their meaning and interpretation. It is the person of Jesus who spoke, and the person of the worshipper who responds, directly, immediately, and in a time that is the stuff of life as lived rather than history.

To say that the liturgy occurs in a perceived time of which the worshipper is the perceiver is as much as can be said within the context of something that calls itself an antitheology. From the perspective of classic metaphysical theology this might seem like settling for less, a lot less than any committed believer has a right to expect. We can, if we wish, throw away the ladder of baby steps it provides in favor of the more expansive advantages of metaphysics. To do so, however, is to forever forsake the directness and simplicity of some of life's most basic but least metaphysical experiences, to ignore "what is the case." To understand oneself as taking up the terms of a personal request made across the ages is nothing more or less than understanding oneself as a follower of that person, a role Kierkegaard epitomized as that of the "contemporary disciple." Historically doctrines may appear, develop, and grow obsolete or irrelevant, but the text of the request, difficult as it is, remains.

BIBLIOGRAPHY

Adam, Frank. *About Time: Cosmology and Culture at the Twilight of the Big Bang.* New York: Free Press, 2011.
Adams, Marilyn McCord. *Some Later Medieval Theories of the Eucharist.* Oxford: Oxford University Press, 2010.
———. *William Ockham.* 2 vols. Notre Dame: University of Notre Dame Press, 1987.
Adams, Nicholas. *Habermas and Theology.* Cambridge: Cambridge University Press, 2006.
Ambrose of Milan. *Saint Ambrose: Theological and Dogmatic Works.* Translated by R. J. Deferrari. Washington, DC: Catholic University of America Press, 1963.
Anselm of Canterbury. *Anselm of Canterbury: Major Works.* Edited by B. Davies and G. R. Evans. Oxford: Oxford University Press, 1998.
———. *S. Anselmi Cantuariensis Archiepiscopi Opera Omnia.* Edited by F. S. Schmidt. 6 vols. Edinburgh: Thomas Nelson, 1946–68.
———. *Trinity, Incarnation, and Redemption: Theological Treatises.* Translated by J. Hopkins and H. Richardson. New York: Harper & Row, 1970.
———. *Truth, Freedom, and Evil: Three Philosophical Dialogues.* Translated by J. Hopkins and H. Richardson. New York: Harper & Row, 1967.
Aristotle. *Aristotle's Theory of Poetry and Fine Art.* Translated by S. H. Butcher. New York: Dover, 1951.
———. *De generatione et corruptione.* Translated by C. J. F. Williams. Oxford: Clarendon, 1982.
———. *On the Soul; Parva Naturalia; On Breath.* Translated by W. S. Hett. Cambridge, MA: Harvard University Press, 1957.
———. *The Rhetoric of Aristotle.* Translated by Lane Cooper. Englewood Cliffs, NJ: Prentice-Hall, 1960.
Augustine. *Christian Doctrine.* Translated by D. W. Robertson Jr. Indianapolis: Bobbs-Merrill, 1958.
———. *Confessions.* Translated by R. S. Pine-Coffin. London: Penguin, 1961.
———. *De dialectica.* Translated by B. D. Jackson. Dordrecht: D. Reidel, 1975.
———. *The Essential Augustine.* Edited by V. J. Bourke. Indianapolis: Hackett, 1974.
———. *The Literal Meaning of Genesis.* Translated by J. H. Taylor. New York: Paulist, 1982.
———. *On the Trinity.* In *Nicene and Post-Nicene Fathers,* edited by Philp Schaff, 3:17–228. Grand Rapids: Eerdmans, 1956.
Austin, J. L. *How to Do Things with Words.* Edited by J. O. Urmson. New York: Oxford University Press, 1965.

Bibliography

———. *Philosophical Papers*. Edited by J. O. Urmson and G. J. Warnock. 2nd ed. New York: Oxford University Press, 1970.
Badiou, Alain. *Being and Event*. Translated by Oliver Feltham. London: Continuum, 2005.
———. *Deleuze: The Clamor of Being*. Translated by L. Burchill. Minneapolis: University of Minnesota Press, 2000.
———. *Logics of Worlds: Being and Event II*. Translated by Alberto Toscano. London: Continuum, 2009.
———. *Saint Paul: The Foundation of Universalism*. Translated by R. Brassier. Stanford: Stanford University Press, 2003.
———. *Theory of the Subject*. Translated by B. Bosteels. London: Continuum, 2009.
———. *Wittgenstein's Antiphilosophy*. Translated by B. Bosteels. London: Verso, 2011.
Balthasar, Hans Urs von. *Presence and Thought: Essay on the Religious Philosophy of Gregory of Nyssa*. Translated by M. Sebanc. San Francisco: Ignatius, 1995.
Barbour, Julian. *The End of Time: The Next Revolution in Our Understanding of the Universe*. New York: Oxford University Press, 1999.
Barth, Karl. *Anselm: Fides Quaerens Intellectum*. Translated by I. W. Robertson. Cleveland: World Publishing, 1962.
Beckwith, Sarah, ed. *Catholicism and Catholicity: Eucharistic Communities in Historical and Contemporary Perspectives*. Oxford: Blackwell, 1999.
Benjamin, Walter. *Illuminations*. Translated by H. Zohn. New York: Harcourt, Brace, 1968.
Bolton, F. R. *The Caroline Tradition of the Church of Ireland, with Special Reference to Bishop Jeremy Taylor*. London: SPCK, 1958.
Bouyer, Louis. *Eucharist: Theology and Spirituality of the Eucharistic Prayer*. Translated by C. U. Quinn. Notre Dame: University of Notre Dame Press, 1968.
Browe, Peter. *Die Eucharistischen Wunder des Mittelalters*. Breslau: Müller & Seifert, 1938.
Bultmann, Rudolf. *The Gospel of John: A Commentary*. Translated by G. R. Beasley-Murray. Philadelphia: Westminster, 1971.
———. *Theology of the New Testament*. Vol. 1. Translated by K. Grobel. New York: Scribner's, 1951.
Buridan, John. *Summulae de Dialectica*. Translated by G. Klima. New Haven: Yale University Press, 2001.
Bynum, Carolyn Walker. *Christian Materiality: An Essay on Religion in Late Medieval Europe*. New York: Zone, 2011.
———. "Seeing and Seeing Beyond: The Mass of St. Gregory in the Fifteenth Century." In *The Mind's Eye: Art and Theological Argument in the Middle Ages*, edited by Jeffrey K. Hamburger, 208–40. Princeton: Princeton University Press, 2005.
Calvin, John. *Institutes of the Christian Religion*. Edited by John T. McNeill. Translated by Ford Lewis Battles. 2 vols. Philadelphia: Westminster, 1960.
Caputo, John D. *The Weakness of God: A Theology of the Event*. Bloomington: Indiana University Press, 2006.
Chemnitz, Martin. *Loci Theologici*. Translated by J. A. O. Preus. St. Louis: Concordia, 1989.
Chenu, M.-D. *Toward Understanding St. Thomas*. Translated by A.-M. Landry and D. Hughes. Chicago: Henry Regnery, 1964.
Clement of Alexandria. *Christ the Educator*. Edited by Roy J. Deferrari. Translated by S. P. Wood. The Fathers of the Church: A New Translation 23. Washington, DC: Catholic University of America Press, 1954.
Conzelmann, Hans. *1 Corinthians: A Commentary on the First Epistle to the Corinthians*. Translated by J. W. Leitch. Philadelphia: Fortress, 1975.

Bibliography

Cowdrey, H. E. J. *Lanfranc: Scholar, Monk, and Archbishop*. Oxford: Oxford University Press, 2003.

Cross, Richard. *The Physics of Duns Scotus*. Oxford: Clarendon, 1998.

Cullmann, Oscar. *Early Christian Worship*. Translated by A. S. Todd and J. B. Torrance. London: SCM, 1953.

———. *The Johannine Circle*. Translated by John Bowden. Philadelphia: Westminster, 1975.

Cullmann, Oscar, and F. J. Leenhardt. *Essays on the Lord's Supper*. Translated by J. G. Davies. Richmond, VA: John Knox, 1960.

Curtius, Ernst Robert. *European Literature and the Latin Middle Ages*. Translated by W. R. Trask. Princeton: Princeton University Press, 1983.

Davidson, Donald. "The Individuation of Events." In *Essays on Action and Events*, 163–80. 2nd ed. Oxford: Oxford University Press, 2001.

Deleuze, Gilles. *Difference and Repetition*. Translated by Paul Patton. New York: Columbia University Press, 1994.

Denery, Dallas G. *Seeing and Being Seen in the Later Medieval World: Optics, Theology and Religious Life*. Cambridge: Cambridge University Press, 2005.

Depoortere, Frederiek. *Badiou and Theology*. London: T. & T. Clark, 2009.

Derrida, Jacques. "Plato's Pharmacy." In *Dissemination*, 61–171. Translated by Barbara Johnson. Chicago: University of Chicago Press, 1981.

———. *Speech and Phenomena: And Other Essays on Husserl's Theory of Signs*. Translated by D. B. Allison. Evanston, IL: Northwestern University Press, 1973.

Dobell, Brian. *Augustine's Intellectual Conversion: The Journey from Platonism to Christianity*. Cambridge: Cambridge University Press, 2009.

Duns Scotus, John. *Duns Scotus on the Will and Morality*. Translated by A. B. Wolter. Washington, DC: Catholic University of America Press, 1997.

———. *God and Creatures: The Quodlibetal Questions*. Translated by F. Alluntis and A. Wolter. Princeton: Princeton University Press, 1975.

———. *Philosophical Writings: A Selection*. Translated by A. Wolter. Indianapolis: Bobbs-Merrill, 1964.

———. *A Treatise on God as First Principle*. Translated by A. Wolter. Chicago: Franciscan Herald, 1966.

Durkheim, Emile. *The Elementary Forms of Religious Life*. Translated by K. E. Fields. New York: Free Press, 1995.

Eagleton, Terry. *Reason, Faith, and Revolution: Reflections on the God Debate*. New Haven: Yale University Press, 2009.

Eisenstein, Elizabeth L. *The Printing Press as an Agent of Change: Communications and Cultural Transformations in Early Modern Europe*. Cambridge: Cambridge University Press, 1979.

Eriugena, Johannes Scotus. *Periphyseon: On the Division of Nature*. Translated by M. L. Uhlfelder. Indianapolis: Bobbs-Merrill, 1976.

Eusebius. *The History of the Church from Christ to Constantine*. Translated by G. A. Williamson. London: Penguin, 1989.

Evans, G. R. *Anselm*. Danbury, CT: Morehouse-Barlow, 1989.

Fairweather, Eugene R., ed. *A Scholastic Miscellany: Anselm to Ockham*. Philadelphia: Westminster, 1956.

Frei, Hans W. *The Eclipse of Biblical Narrative*. New Haven: Yale University Press, 1974.

Bibliography

———. *Types of Theology*. Edited by G. Hunsinger and W. C. Placher. New Haven: Yale University Press, 1992.
Gallop, D. "Plato and the Alphabet." *Philosophical Review* 72 (1963) 364–76.
Ganz, David. *Corbie in the Carolingian Renaissance*. Sigmaringen, Ger.: Jan Thorbecke, 1990.
Garrigan, Siobhán. *Beyond Ritual*. Burlington, VT: Ashgate, 2004.
Geertz, Clifford. *Local Knowledge: Further Essays in Interpretive Antropology*. New York: Basic Books, 1985.
Geiselmann, Joseph Rupert. *Die Eucharistielehre der Vorscholastik*. Paderborn: Schöningh, 1926.
Grant, Robert M. *Miracle and Natural Law in Graeco-Roman and Early Christian Thought*. Amsterdam: North Holland, 1952.
Guitmund of Aversa. "On the Truth of the Body and Blood of Christ in the Eucharist." In *Lanfranc of Canterbury and Guidmund of Aversa*, 91–217. Translated by M. G. Vaillancourt. Fathers of the Church: Medieval Continuation 10. Washington, DC: Catholic University of America Press, 2009.
Habermas, Jürgen. *Communication and the Evolution of Society*. Translated by T. McCarthy. Boston: Beacon, 1979.
———. *Knowledge and Human Interests*. Translated by J. J. Shapiro. Boston: Beacon, 1971.
———. *On the Logic of the Social Sciences*. Translated by S. W. Nicholsen and J. A. Stark. Cambridge, MA: MIT Press, 1988.
———. *Postmetaphysical Thinking*. Translated by W. M. Hohengarten. Cambridge, MA: MIT Press, 1992.
———. *The Theory of Communicative Action*. Vol. 1, *Reason and the Rationalization of Society*. Translated by T. McCarthy. Boston: Beacon, 1984.
———. *The Theory of Communicative Action*. Vol. 2, *Lifeworld and System: A Critique of Functionalist Reason*. Translated by T. McCarthy. Boston: Beacon, 1987.
Hamburger, Jeffrey F., and A.-M. Bouché, eds. *The Mind's Eye: Art and Theological Argument in the Middle Ages*. Princeton: Princeton University Press, 2006.
Heaney, James J. "A Different Kind of Memorial." *Religion in Life* (Winter 1977) 450–59.
———. "Faith and the Logic of Seeing-As." *International Journal for the Philosophy of Religion* 10 (1979) 189–98.
———. "The Logic of Questions and the Existence of God." *Religious Studies* 16 (1980) 203–16.
Hector, Kevin W. *Theology Without Metaphysics: God, Language and the Spirit of Recognition*. Cambridge: Cambridge University Press, 2011.
Hick, John. "Religious Faith as Experiencing-As." In *Royal Institute of Philosophy Lectures*, edited by the Royal Institute of Philosophy, 2:20–35. London: Macmillan, 1969.
Hirsch, E. D., Jr. *Validity in Interpretation*. New Haven: Yale University Press, 1967.
Holifield, E. Brooks. *The Covenant Sealed: The Development of Puritan Sacramental Theology in Old and New England, 1570–1720*. New Haven: Yale University Press, 1974.
Holland, A. J. "An Argument in Plato's *Theaetetus*: 184–6." *Philosophical Quarterly* 23 (1973) 97–116.
Hopkins, Jasper. *A Companion to the Study of St. Anselm*. Minneapolis: University of Minnesota Press, 1972.
Hunsinger, George. *The Eucharist and Ecumenism: Let Us Keep the Feast*. Cambridge: Cambridge University Press, 2008.

Bibliography

Irvine, Martin. *The Making of Textual Culture: "Grammatica" and Literary Theory, 350-1100.* Cambridge: Cambridge University Press, 1994.
Irwin, Kevin W. *Models of the Eucharist.* New York: Paulist, 2005.
James, William. *The Varieties of Religious Experience: A Study in Human Nature.* New York: New American Library, 1958.
Jeremias, Joachim. *The Eucharistic Words of Jesus.* Translated by Norman Perrin. London: SCM, 1966.
John of the Cross. *Dark Night of the Soul.* Translated by E. Allison Peers. New York: Doubleday, 1990.
Jorissen, Hans. *Die Entfaltung der Transsubstantiationslehre bis zum Beginn der Hochscholastik.* Munster: Aschendorffsche Verlagsbuchhandlung, 1965.
Kant, Immanuel. *Critique of Pure Reason.* Translated by Norman Kemp Smith. New York: St. Martin's, 1965.
———. *Religion Within the Limits of Reason Alone.* Translated by T. M. Greene and H. H. Hudson. New York: Harper, 1960.
Keener, Craig S. *1-2 Corinthians.* Cambridge: Cambridge University Press, 2005.
Kierkegaard, Søren. *Concluding Unscientific Postscript to the Philosophical Fragments.* Translated by D. V. Swenson. Princeton: Princeton University Press, 1968.
———. *Fear and Trembling/Repetition.* Translated by H. V. Hong and E. H. Hong. Princeton: Princeton University Press, 1983.
———. *Philosophical Fragments or A Fragment of Philosophy.* Translated by D. F. Swenson and H. V. Hong. Princeton: Princeton University Press, 1967.
———. *Repetition: An Essay in Experimental Psychology.* Translated by W. Lowrie. New York: Harper & Row, 1941.
Kim, Jaegwon. *Supervenience and Mind: Selected Philosophical Essays.* Cambridge: Cambridge University Press, 1993.
Kneale, W., and M. Kneale. *The Development of Logic.* Oxford: Clarendon, 1962.
Kuhn, Thomas S. *The Structure of Scientific Revolutions.* 2nd ed. Chicago: University of Chicago Press, 1970.
Lamm, Julia A. "The Art of Interpreting Plato." In *The Cambridge Companion to Friedrich Schleiermacher,* edited by J. Mariña, 91-108. Cambridge: Cambridge University Press, 2005.
Lanfranc. "On the Body and Blood of the Lord." In *Lanfranc of Canterbury and Guitmund of Aversa,* 29-87. Translated by M. G. Vaillancourt. The Fathers of the Church: Medieval Continuation 10. Washington, DC: Catholic University of America Press, 2009.
Law, Vivien. *Grammar and Grammarians in the Early Middle Ages.* London: Longman, 1997.
Lawrence, of the Resurrection. *Brother Lawrence: The Practice of the Presence of God the Best Rule of a Holy Life.* New York: Revell, 1895.
Leach, Edmund R. "Genesis as Myth." In *Myth and Cosmos: Readings in Mythology and Symbolism,* edited by John Middleton, 1-13. Austin: University of Texas Press, 1967.
Lévi-Strauss, Claude. "Four Winnebago Myths." In *Myth and Cosmos: Readings in Mythology and Symbolism,* edited by John Middleton, 15-26. Austin: University of Texas Press, 1967.
Lindbeck, George A. *The Nature of Doctrine: Religion and Theology in a Postliberal Age.* Philadelphia: Westminster, 1984.

Bibliography

Lindberg, David C. *The Beginnings of Western Science: The European Scientific Tradition in Philosophical, Religious, and Institutional Context, Prehistory to A.D. 1450*. 2nd ed. Chicago: University of Chicago Press, 2007.

———. *Theories of Vision from al-Kindi to Kepler*. Chicago: University of Chicago Press, 1976.

Longinus. "On the Sublime." In *Classical Literary Criticism*, 99–158. Translated by T. S. Dorsch. Harmondsworth, UK: Penguin, 1965.

Lubac, Henri de. *Corpus Mysticum: The Eucharist and the Church in the Middle Ages*. Translated by Gemma Simmons. Notre Dame: University of Notre Dame Press, 2007.

Luhtala, Anneli. "Syntax and Dialectic in Carolingian Commentaries on Priscian's *Institutiones grammaticae*." In *History of Linguistic Thought in the Early Middle Ages*, edited by Vivien Law, 151–54. Philadelphia: John Benjamins, 1993.

Macy, Gary. *The Theologies of the Eucharist in the Early Scholastic Period*. Oxford: Clarendon, 1984.

Manoussakis, John Panteleimon. *God after Metaphysics: A Theological Aesthetic*. Bloomington: Indiana University Press, 2007.

Marion, Jean-Luc. *God Without Being: Hors-Texte*. Translated by T. A. Carlson. Chicago: University of Chicago Press, 1991.

Marmion, D., and R. Van Nieuwenhove. *An Introduction to the Trinity*. Cambridge: Cambridge University Press, 2011.

McDonnell, Kilian. *John Calvin, the Church, and the Eucharist*. Princeton: Princeton University Press, 1967.

McTaggert, J. E. "The Unreality of Time." *Mind: A Quarterly Review of Psychology and Philosophy* 17 (1908) 457–74.

Melancthon, Philip. *Melancthon on Christian Doctrine: Loci Communes 1555*. Translated by C. L. Manschreck. New York: Oxford University Press, 1965.

Morgan, David. *The Sacred Gaze: Religious Visual Culture in Theory and Practice*. Berkeley: University of California Press, 2005.

Murphy-O'Connor, Jerome. *Keys to First Corinthians: Revisiting the Major Issues*. Oxford: Oxford University Press, 2010.

Nicholas of Cusa. "Letter to Kaspar Ayndorffer." In *The Essential Writings of Christian Mysticism*, edited by B. McGinn, 270–72. New York: Modern Library, 2006.

Nestroy, Johann Nepomuk. "The Talisman: Farce with Song in Three Acts." In *Three Viennese Comedies*, translated by R. Harrison and K. Wilson, 15–92. Columbia, SC: Camden, 1986.

Nielsen, Kai, and D. Z. Phillips. *Wittgensteinian Fideism?* London: SCM, 2011.

Oberman, Heiko A. *The Harvest of Medieval Theology: Gabriel Biel and Late Medieval Nominalism*. Grand Rapids: Eerdmans, 1967.

Otto, Rudolf. *The Idea of the Holy: An Inquiry into the Non-Rational Factor in the Idea of the Divine and Its Relation to the Rational*. Translated by J. W. Harvey. New York: Oxford University Press, 1958.

Pascasius Radbertus. "The Lord's Body and Blood." In *Early Medieval Theology*, 90–117. Translated by G. E. McCracken and A. Cabaniss. Library of Christian Classics 9. Philadelphia: Westminster, 1957.

———. *Paschasius Radbertus. De corpore et sanguine Domini*. Edited by Bede Paulus. Corpus Christianorum, Continuatio Medievalis 16. Turnhout, Belg.: Brepols, 1969.

Pasnau, Robert. "Cognition." In *The Cambridge Companion to Duns Scotus*, edited by Thomas Williams, 288–90. Cambridge: Cambridge University Press, 2003.

Bibliography

Passalacqua, Marina. "Priscian's *Institutio de nomine et pronomine et verbo* in the Ninth Century." In *History of Linguistic Thought in the Early Middle Ages*, edited by Vivien Law, 195-96. Philadelphia: John Benjamins, 1993.

Pelikan, Jaroslav. *The Christian Tradition*. Vol. 1, *The Emergence of the Catholic Tradition (100-600)*. Chicago: University of Chicago Press, 1971.

———. *Jesus Through the Centuries: His Place in the History of Culture*. New Haven: Yale University Press, 1985.

Phelps, Hollis. *Alain Badiou: Between Theology and Anti-Theology*. Durham, UK: Acumen, 2013.

Phillips, D. Z. *The Concept of Prayer*. New York: Seabury, 1981.

Philo Judaeus. *The Essential Philo*. Edited by Nahum Glatzer. New York: Schocken, 1971.

Pianesi, Fabio, and Achille C. Varzi. "Events and Events Talk: An Introduction." In *Speaking of Events*, edited by J. Higginbotham, F. Pianesi, and A. C. Varzi, 3-48. New York: Oxford University Press, 2000.

Pickstock, Catherine. *After Writing: On the Liturgical Consummation of Philosophy*. Oxford: Blackwell, 1998.

Plato. *The Collected Dialogues of Plato*. Edited by E. Hamilton and H. Cairns. New York: Pantheon, 1961.

Polkinghorne, John. *Belief in God in an Age of Science*. New Haven: Yale University Press, 1998.

Powers, Joseph M. *Eucharistic Theology*. New York: Seabury, 1967.

Ratramnus of Corbie. "Christ's Body and Blood." In *Early Medieval Theology*, 109-47. Translated by G. E. McCracken and A. Cabaniss. Library of Christian Classics 9. Philadelphia: Westminster, 1957.

———. *Ratramnus de corpore et sanguine domini: Texte établi d'après les manuscrits et notice bibliographique*. Edited by N. Bakhuizen van de Brink. Amsterdam: North-Holland, 1954.

Ratzinger, Joseph. *God Is Near Us: The Eucharist, the Heart of Life*. Edited by S. O. Horn and V. Pfnür. Translated by H. Taylor. San Francisco: Ignatius, 2003.

Recht, Roland. *Believing and Seeing: The Art of Gothic Cathedrals*. Translated by M. Whittall. Chicago: University of Chicago Press, 2008.

Reichenbach, Hans. *Elements of Symbolic Logic*. New York: Free Press, 1947.

Rubin, Miri. *Corpus Christi: The Eucharist in Late Medieval Culture*. Cambridge: Cambridge University Press, 1991.

Ryle, Gilbert. "Letters and Syllables in Plato." *Philosophical Review* 69 (1960) 431-51.

Saliers, Don E. "'Taste and See': Sacramental Renewal among United Methodists." *Quarterly Review: A Journal of Theological Resources for Ministry* 22 (2002) 223-33.

Schillebeeckx, Edward. *The Eucharist*. Translated by N. D. Smith. New York: Sheed and Ward, 1968.

Schneider, John R. *Philip Melanchthon's Rhetorical Construal of Biblical Authority—Oratio Sacra*. Lewiston, NY: E. Mellen, 1990.

Schweitzer, Albert. *The Problem of the Lord's Supper*. Translated by A. J. Mattill Jr. Macon, GA: Mercer University Press, 1982.

———. *The Quest of the Historical Jesus*. Translated by W. Montgomery. New York: Macmillan, 1961.

Searle, John R. *Expression and Meaning: Studies in the Theory of Speech Acts*. Cambridge: Cambridge University Press, 1979.

Bibliography

———. *Intentionality: An Essay in the Philosophy of Mind*. Cambridge: Cambridge University Press, 1983.

———. *Mind: A Brief Introduction*. Oxford: Oxford University Press, 2004.

———. *The Social Construction of Reality*. New York: Free Press, 1995.

Smalley, Beryl. *The Study of the Bible in the Middle Ages*. Notre Dame: University of Notre Dame Press, 1964.

Stalnaker, Robert J. "Pragmatics." *Synthese* 22 (1970) 272–89.

Staniforth, M., and A. Louth, trans. *The Apostolic Fathers: Early Christian Writings*. London: Penguin, 1968.

Stock, Brian. *The Implications of Literacy: Written Language and Models of Interpretation in the Eleventh and Twelfth Centuries*. Princeton: Princeton University Press, 1983.

Taylor, Jeremy. *Holy Living and Holy Dying*. Vol. 1, *Holy Living*. Edited by P. G. Stanwood. Oxford: Clarendon, 1989.

———. *The Whole Works of Jeremy Taylor, D.D.* Edited by Reginald Heber. 3rd ed. of the collected works. London: Longman, Orme, Brown, Green, and Longmans, 1839.

Thérèse of Lisieux. *Story of a Soul: The Autobiography of Saint*. Translated by J. Clarke. 3rd ed. Washington: ICS, 1996.

Thomas à Kempis. *The Imitation of Christ*. Translated by L. Sherley-Price. Harmondsworth, UK: Penguin, 1952.

Thomas Aquinas. *Corpus Thomisticum, Sancti Thomae de Aquino: Summa Theologiae*. 1888 Leonine edition. http://www.corpusthomisticum.org/sth1002.html.

———. *Summa Theologiae*. Blackfriars edition. New York: McGraw-Hill, 1964—.

Thurian, Max. *The Eucharistic Memorial*. Translated by J. G. Davies. 2 vols. Richmond, VA: John Knox, 1960, 1961.

Trochu, Francis. *The Curé d'Ars: A Shorter Biography*. Translated by R. Matthews. London: Burns & Oates, 1955.

Vaillancourt, M. G. *Lanfranc of Canterbury and Guidmund of Aversa*. Washington, DC: Catholic University of America Press, 2009.

Wallace-Hadrill, J. M. *The Frankish Church*. Oxford: Clarendon, 1983.

William of Ockham. *The De Sacramento Altaris of William of Ockham*. Translated by T. Bruce Birch. Eugene, OR: Wipf & Stock, 2009.

Williams, Thomas, ed. *The Cambridge Companion to Duns Scotus*. Cambridge: Cambridge University Press, 2003.

Wimsatt, W. K., and M. C. Beardsley. *The Verbal Icon: Studies in the Meaning of Poetry*. Lexington: University of Kentucky Press, 1967.

Wittgenstein, Ludwig. *Notebooks, 1914–1916*. Translated by G. E. M. Anscombe. New York: Harper, 1961.

———. *On Certainty*. Translated by G. E. M. Anscombe and G. H. von Wright. New York: Harper, 1969.

———. *Philosophical Investigations*. Translated by G. E. M. Anscombe. New York: Macmillan, 1953.

———. *Tractatus Logico-Philosophicus*. Translated by D. F. Pears and B. V. McGuinness. London: Routledge & Kegan Paul, 1961.

Wrathall, Mark A., ed. *Religion after Metaphysics*. Cambridge: Cambridge University Press, 2003.

Yates, Frances A. *Giordano Bruno and the Hermetic Tradition*. New York: Routledge, 1964.

INDEX

accedia, 59
Adams, Marilyn McCord, 19n8, 41n78
affective fallacy, 47, 82
alphabet, as means of "seeing-through," 39
Ambrose, Saint, 17n4, 30
analogy, doctrine of, 139
anaphora, Eucharistic, 56, 73, 95–97, 101–4
  as performative utterance, 75
  and *passim*
Anselm of Canterbury
  de Veritate, 9
  faith seeking understanding, 1
  "Letters on the Sacraments," 9
  Monologion, 5
  ontological argument, 2–3
  Proslogion, 4
  Why God Became Man, 2
antiphilosophy, 7
antitheology, 6–8, 13–14, 117–19
Aristotle, 84–85
  Poetics, 62
  On Interpretation, 74
Arndt, Johann, *True Christianity*, 8
assertions, locutionary 74
  performative, 74–91
Augustine of Hippo
  on Eucharist as cannibalism, 96
  on Genesis, 36n61
  on hallucinatory seeing, 39
  literary style, 2
  on locutionary speech, 74
  on self-knowledge, 123

Austin, J. L., 74
  on performative utterances, 74–79

Badiou, Alain, 7, 85–89, 92, 99, 103
  and "dialectical idealism," 117–18
  on Deleuze, 61n41
Balthasar, Hans Urs von, 123n30
Barth, Karl, 3n4
Benjamin, Walter, 106
Berengarius of Tours, 31n43, 107
  condemned at Synod of Vercelli, 1050
Bergson, Henri, 18
Berlin, Königstädter theatre, 65, 67
Bible, "Wicked," 91n33
biblicism, 45–47
Boethius, 33–34
Brother Lawrence of the Resurrection. *See* Herman, Nicholas
Buridan, John, on intentionality, 139n63
Bynum, Carolyn Walker, 37
  on materiality as medieval paradigm, 41

Calvin, John, 114
  grace and inspiration in interpretation, 46–47
  on Eucharistic words as metonymy, 110–11
Cano, Melchior, 114
category mistake, 90
categories, Kantian, 60
change, Eucharistic, 33, 38
Chemnitz, Martin, 104

Index

Cicero, and forensic argument in the Reformation, 115
Clement of Alexandria, 109
Communion, Holy, 128
conditions of possible understanding (Habermas), 100–101
criticism, biblical, 16, 45–48
   Kant on, 46n3
Curé d'Ars. *see* John Vianney, saint

d'Ailly, Pierre, 140
Davidson, Donald, 84
Deleuze, Gilles, 61n41, 91
demonstration, method of, 112
Der Talisman, 65–68
Derridas, Jacques, 123–24
Descartes, René, 92
dialectic, Hegelian, 60
Didache, 110–11
différance, 16, 68
Duns Scotus, John, on the univocity of being, 29–30,140
Durkheim, Émile, 77

Edwards, Jonathan, 8
Ethical, the, Kierkegaardian category, 69–70
Eucharist
   as substance, 10, 12
   "medicine of immortality," 70
   unworthy reception of, 96
experiential-expressive use of language, 82

farce, 67, 69–70
fidelity, Badiou concept of, 86–87, 97
Fourth Lateran Council, 30
Freud, and personal identity, 13

Garrigan, Siobhán, 100–102
Geertz, Clifford, 17
   Local Knowledge, 19
Gilson, Étienne, 3n4
grammatical studies, Carolingian, 32–35
Grammaticus, Vergilius Maro, on reading as "seeing-through," 37
Gregory Mass, 37, 127
Guitmund of Aversa, 9–10

Habermas, Jürgen, 14, 77–78, 101
   on "worlds," 83
Hamann, Johan Georg, quoted by Kierkegaard, 92
happiness, as quality of a speech act, 80–81, 83, 97, 123
Herman, Nicholas, 135–36, 138, 144
Hirsch, E. D., on consciousness and meaning, 82n18
Hrabanus Maurus, opposition to physicality of Radbertus, 41
Hume, David, 6
   on causality, 60
Husserl, Edmund, 123–24
hypostasis, 122

identity, principle of, 28–29
Ignatius of Antioch, Eucharist as "medicine of immortality," 70
intention
   "first," and "second," 139
   of a speaker, 81–83
   original 82
intentional fallacy, 47
intentionality, 130–34, 139
   and time, 133–34
intervention, 69
   the Moment as, 68
intervention, 86, 90
Irvine, Martin, on polysemy of text, 48n12
Isidore of Seville, 73

James, William, *Varieties of Religious Experience*, 129–30
Jastrow, Joseph, optical puzzles, 20
John Vianney, saint, 127–28

Kant, Immanuel, 6, 60
Kierkegaard, Søren, 90–94, 99
   Constantine Constantius, pseudonymous author, 66
   Fear and Trembling, 58, 75, 93
   on relation of faith to history, 134–35, 140, 143–44
   on repetition, 125
   on "the contemporary disciple," 59
   Philosophical Fragments, 68

Index

Repetition, 58–69
the "interesting," 16–17, 19, 39
Kuhn, Thomas, 42
 Structure of Scientific Revolutions, 19–20

Lanfranc of Bec, 9
language, doxological, 145
 figurative, 108–11
 performative, 83
 theories of pragmatic use, 76n8
lectio divina, 3
lifeworld, 42, 103
 of utterances, 83
Lindberg, David, 23n21
liturgical movement, 12, 126
loci, 124
 as basis of argument, 115–16
Logical Positivism, 6–7, 19n8, 76n8
logos, as "account" in Plato, 5
Lucian of Samosata, 52n21
Lucretius, 6

Marion, Jean-Luc, quoted, 56n28
Marx, Karl, 6
"mediation," 60, 92
Melanchthon, Philip, 114–16
Melchisedech, 110
Merleau-Ponty, Maurice, 18
metaphysics, end of, 12
minima and *minima naturalia*, 107
miracles, Eucharistic, 33, 38–41
 in Radbertus, 39–40
Moment, the, 66–70
Morgan, David, 51

Nicholas of Cusa, 140
normal, natural, ordinary, 88, 90, 99
"now," 84–85

Otto, Rudolf, *Idea of the Holy*, 130

Papias of Hierapolis, 44
paradigm shift, 20–22, 30–43
Pascal, Blaise, 88–89
"Pascasian Canon," 42
Passover Meal, 95–96
Pelikan, Jaroslav, 55

performance, dramatic, 67
performative utterances. *see* utterances, performative
persona, as translating Gr. *prosopon*, 122
Philo Judaeus, 109
Pickstock, Catherine, 145
Pietism, 7–8
Plato, 99
 on writing, 49–50, 53
 Phaedrus, 13, 49–50, 71
 Theaetetus, 52–54
Platonism, 29
presence
 concept of, 124–34
 of God, 135
presence
 Eucharistic, by natural concomitance, 108, 125
 figurative, 35–38
 personal, 122–24
 real, 12, 120–22
presupposition, 93, 97–98, 101
 of a speech act, 79–80, 94–95
Priscian, 34n40, 36
promises, false, 81–83
puzzles, optical, 20–21

quotation, as performative, 90–92

Radbertus of Corbie, 31–38
Ratramnus of Corbie, 31–38, 96, 109
recollection, 58–60, 66–68
red-letter text, 51
Reichenbach, Hans, on pragmatic language, 80n15
remembrance, Eucharistic, 71
repetition, 103–5
 concept of, 57–66
 Eucharistic, 124–25
 vs. re-enactment, 62
requests, as performative, 87–88
 text of, 88
Rubin, Miri, 33n48

sacramental action, *ex opere operato*, 59
Sacrifice of the Cross, 110
Schillebeekx, Edward, on transubstantiation, 18

157

Index

Schleiermacher, Friedrich, 55
Schweitzer, Albert, 55
Scotus Erigena, Ratramnus mistaken for, 41
Searle, John, 14, 76–77
   on intentionality, 131n43
Second Vatican Council, 18
seeing-as, 21–22, 28–29
semiotic anxiety, 48
singularity, 86
situation
   Badiou on, 86
   liturgical, 101–2
   of a speech act, 79–83
speech act, 74
   as event, 83–89
   performative, 122–23
   requirements for, 79
   schematized, 78
   text of, 89–94
Stolz, Anselm, 3n4
Strauss, D. F., 8
substance, 37–38, 41–42
   and *ousia*, 41n78
   as intellectual category, 120
   ninth-century notions of, 34
synoptic gospels, on words of institution, 17

Tarquin the Proud, 92
Taylor, Jeremy, 8, 136–41, 144
Teilhard de Chardin, Pierre, 8
text
   and Revelation, 118–19
   and ritual, 61
   and the Moment, 67
   and tradition, 55–57
   as presupposition, 97–98
   criticism of, 63
   redundancy of, 61
theology, associative, 112–17
   rationalist, 111–13
Thérèse of Lisieux, saint, 128–29
Thomas Aquinas, 108, 112–14
   Five Ways to the existence of God, 5–6
   on Eucharistic miracles, 33
time, and liturgy, 146
   "arrow of," 141
   "perceived," 142
   reality of 142
   recorded or "factual," 142–43
   transcended, 88–89
token-reflexive expressions, 78
topics. See *loci*
transelementation, 126n126
translational fallacy, 47–48
transubstantiation, 11, 18–19, 30–32, 41–42, 77
Trent, Council of, 18, 30, 42, 107, 119, 127
truth (*veritas*) vs. figure (*figura*), 35–38
type or prefigurement, 110

United Methodist Church on Eucharistic presence, 126n33
utterances, performative, 74–76, 87

vere, realiter, substantialiter, 107
Vincentian Canon, 18
vision, Aristotle on, 23–24
   as paradigm for intellect, 22–23
   extramissive theory, 24–30
   in Augustine 27
   in Origen, 26
   in Philo Judaeus, 26
   in *Republic*, 25–26
   in *Timaeus*, 21,
   intromissive theory, 24–25, 29
Void, the, Badiou, 85–86

William of Ockham, 32
   "razor," 46
Wittgenstein, Ludwig, 6, 15, 57, 83
   on language games, 21
   Platonizing questions of, 117–18n22
   seeing-as, 20–21
   world as "what is the case," 138
words of institution. See anaphora, Eucharistic
writing, alphabetic vs. hieroglyphic, 51–52

www.ingramcontent.com/pod-product-compliance
Lightning Source LLC
Chambersburg PA
CBHW050820160426
43192CB00010B/1828